Emergency Income Streams:
How to Create Fast Cash in 14 Days or Less

By Kristi Patrice Carter, JD

Emergency Income Streams: How to Create Fast Cash in 14 Days or Less

© 2016 Kristi Patrice Carter, JD

All rights reserved. No part of this book may be reproduced or transmitted in any form or by any means, electronic or mechanical, including photocopying, recording, or by any information storage and retrieval system, without written permission of the publisher, except in the case of brief quotations embodied in articles or reviews.

Disclaimer

NOTE FROM THE AUTHOR

This book is designed to provide factual information in regard to the subject matter covered. However, it is based on personal experience, interviews with other multiple-income seekers, and research conducted by the author and her freelance staff. Although much effort was made to ensure that all information in the book is factual and accurate, this book is sold with the understanding that the author assumes no responsibility for oversights, discrepancies, or inaccuracies. This book is not intended to replace financial, investment, legal, accounting, or other professional services. If these services are required, a competent professional should be sought. Readers are reminded to use their own good judgment before applying any ideas presented in this book.

For information, contact:

Thang Publishing Company
332 South Michigan Avenue, Suite 1032, #T610
Chicago, IL 60604-4434

http://www.thangpublishing.com

For information on additional income stream opportunities, visit:
http://www.incomestreams.guru

Table of Contents

Acknowledgments 1
Introduction 3
#1: Unclaimed Property 9
#2: About Those Annoying Creditors: Contact Them Now! 17
#3: Loans 29
#4: Selling Stuff 40
#5: Make Emergency Money with an Online and Off-Line Garage Sale 44
#6: Making Emergency Money with an Online Garage Sale 47
#7: How to Make Emergency Money Engaging in eBay Retail Arbitrage 54
#8: Getting Hired to Make Emergency Money 57
#9: How to Make Extra Money by Finding a Job on Craigslist ... 60
#10: How to Make Emergency Money by Working for Temp Agencies 62
#11: How to Make Emergency Money by Doing a Job 64
#12: Selling Services via Freelance Websites Freelancing 66
#13: How to Make Emergency Money by Tutoring 73
#14: Emergency Money as a Babysitter 75
#15: How to Make Emergency Money by Going Door to Door Offering Handyman Services 78
#16 Emergency Money as a Dog Walker or a Pet Sitter 80
#17: Making Emergency Money via Entrepreneurship 83
#18: How to Make Emergency Money by Offering Services to Local Businesses 86
#19: Emergency Money as an Online Bulletin Board Poster for People and/or Businesses Selling Stuff 88

#20: Emergency Money as an Errand Runner 91
#21: Emergency Money as a Housekeeper 95
#22: Emergency Money as a Gardener/Landscaper 98
#23: How to Make Emergency Money as a Pressure Washer 101
#24: How to Make Emergency Money Selling Scrap Metal 104
#25: How to Make More Emergency Money at the Recycling Center 106
#26: A Crazy Idea: 110
#27: A Crazy Idea: 114
#28: A Crazy Idea: 116
Conclusion 118
BONUS 119
About the Author 135

Acknowledgments

This book is dedicated to:

My loving husband and best friend, Delanza Shun-tay Carter, for encouraging me to write this book, for being supportive when I wanted to give up, and for his innate ability to occupy the kids with various activities so I could complete this book.

My daughter, Kristin Carter, and my sons, Shaun Carter and Daniel Carter, for listening as I read my drafts out loud, offering great advice, being willing to eat breakfast for dinner, and encouraging me to "get that book done" so we could do something fun!

My mom, Christina Tarr, who has always offered unwavering love and support, for helping out in every way possible to make my writing dreams a reality, and for encouraging my writing efforts (from my very first story about a sick little girl named Nan who stayed home from school to the crafting of this book many years later).

My father, Lavon Tarr, for loving me, being a great dad, and not complaining when Mom came over.

My grandmother, Fannie Lee Richardson, for her incredible strength, consistent faith, and positive attitude.

My mother-in-law, Michelle Carter, for unselfishly making delicious meals and treats for the family; and my father-in-law, Barney Lee Carter, for picking up the kiddos; and to both of them for always being willing to help out in a pinch to accommodate my writing time.

My best friend, Angela Whitaker-Payton (Moinks); my adopted mom, Darlene Norem-Smith (Mama D); my sister, Dana B. Robinson; Aunt Barbara Rhodes; Aunt Patricia J. Ray (Patty Cake); cousins Alison Turner, Lucy Beal, and Chanda Taylor-Conrad; adopted grand mom, Gladys Crump; and all my other amazing family members and friends (not mentioned here) who encouraged me to write my book and to never give up on my dream of helping others!

My researchers, motivators, idea generators, and best writing buddies, Christy Mossburg and Geradina Tomacruz; my editors, Amy Shelby and Denise Barker; my proofreader, Meredith Dunn; and my graphic designer, Alex, for designing my dynamic eBook cover. Without your assistance, this book would not have been possible.

Finally, and most important, I would like to give a heartfelt thanks to all the emergency income seekers reading this book. I understand that obtaining emergency income isn't easy and takes creativity, skills, effort, commitment, and perseverance. However, if you're willing to put in the work, you will surely reap the benefits of your efforts. I applaud you for taking the first step toward making your financial dreams a reality. You can do this! I've got faith in you!

Introduction

Chin Up: Things Aren't as Bad as They Seem

If you are currently experiencing a financial emergency, then I totally understand how hurt, frustrated, disappointed, and scared you must feel. Having a financial emergency can put anyone, even the calmest and most happy-go-lucky person, over the edge. Lack of finances can cause a plethora of emotions, from peace to fear and/or from hopefulness to hopelessness. Depending on your mind-set, these feelings can change from second to second, minute by minute, and hour by hour.

One moment you may feel like burying your head in the sand, hiding from your creditors, and praying that a miracle will happen to make all your money problems disappear. On the other hand you might feel hopeful and ready to tackle this challenge head-on. A tiny voice may even be telling you that your financial situation is not as bad as it seems and that you can make things right.

Well, I'm here to tell you that the inner voice is right. Although things might seem bad, they are certainly not hopeless. Call me optimistic or just plain crazy, but I'm a firm believer that things happen for a reason (a learning experience probably) and that, although your financial situation may feel out of control, you can take control. You still have the power to change the direction of your financial situation—right now.

So you've made financial mistakes—we all have, but we can't wallow in them. Instead we have to focus on victory. We have to see ourselves as powerful, capable, and competent individuals who will obtain the money we need in a short period of time. But we can't just wish things were different. We have to align our vision with action to make the magic happen. With a winning attitude, optimistic mind-set, action plan, and then followed by our own actions, we can make the money we need.

And how do I know? From experience. Unfortunately I have been where you are right now on more than one occasion. I understand what you're going through. I know the embarrassment and hurt you feel when you aren't prepared for the smallest emergency or when your debit card gets declined yet again simply because you purchased a pack of chewing gum. Not to mention the anger when you get slapped with a $30 overdraft bank fee because you didn't have $1 in your checking account to cover the $0.99 purchase for the above pack of gum. (Yes, this has happened to me, and it was not funny at all.) I also know how terrifying it feels to be faced with credit card collection calls day in and day out and how good it feels to be debt-free and to have enough money in your account to cover everyday essentials, splurges, and then some.

I've been there, and I can tell you firsthand that light is at the end of this dark and lonely financial tunnel. You can get out of this black hole and turn your finances around within fourteen days or less, and you can do it with my fourteen-day action plan. No giving up during these first fourteen days!

I have to be honest with you though. My action plan will take some work, and it won't be easy. It will require that you put in a bit of elbow grease and effort. You may even have to hit the pavement to find a gig that no one else wants to do. But, if you have determination, will, creativity, passion, and are willing to put in the work, you can make cold hard cash. You can get your financial life back on track, one dollar at a time.

Even if you're skeptical, my plan will work and is unlike many other emergency plans that promise to teach you how to get out of a financial mess but only give you scanty information plus an incredible offer to purchase another course. Then, if you do purchase the course, you're left with more questions and no real actionable plan. How do I know? Because I bought hundreds of them when I was in desperate financial situations and was always disappointed by their lack of real advice. But the good news is, this book is not one of those hyped-up crappy offers that doesn't deliver. This book delivers and will teach you proven strategies to make fast cash in fourteen days or less.

Plus, when you combine these strategies with a burning desire to succeed and make things happen, you will feel more empowered and can avoid these situations in the future. And, if for some reason you do slip up again, you'll be better prepared to handle the next emergency. You'll have the confidence to know you can repeat your earlier success.

So, if you're ready to make up to or more than $500 a week, then you need to become committed right now. Pull up your sleeves, put on your creativity moneymaking cap, and get ready to make it happen, baby. We don't have a moment to spare. We've got only fourteen days to make that cash. Fourteen days. Let's do this thang.

Change Your Mind-Set, Change the Outcome

Before we even begin discussing the make-money-fast action plan, we need to be in the right state of mind. Although it may be tempting to panic and feel overwhelmed, don't do it! Or at least only allow yourself to feel negative thoughts for a very short period of time (like five minutes a day—at the most) and then move on to more empowering thoughts. If you wallow in negativity for too long, you'll get frustrated, depressed, and then make bad financial decisions based on those "bad" emotions. Instead you need to turn things around and realize that, although your financial boat may be sinking, you have a life boat: this book. You have a life jacket: your unique skills and qualifications. And finally you have your desires and talents, which equal the ability to swim out of this mess.

Repeat after me:

> I can and will make the money that I need to get myself out of this financial situation. I am resourceful, committed, and confident. I am open and receptive to any ideas or opportunities that present themselves. I know in my heart and soul that I can and will make the money I need in a timely fashion. I accept the money that will soon flow to me, and so it is!

Whenever you feel down and distraught, reread this section. Repeat the above statement of intention until it sinks in—really sinks in. Reread it. Commit it to memory, and say it until you believe it is true.

Now that you're fired up and have your mind tuned to the success channel, let's talk about how to assess what you need and how to fill up your financial hole.

Budgets and Spending Plans

The best way to fill a financial hole is to stop digging a deeper one. Therefore, you need to use a budget or, better yet, a spending plan. Although it's not fun writing down every single bit of income and expenses, it is extremely important that you do this step. Take it from me, having a workable budget or spending plan will keep you on track and will help you set the course right when you get off track.

For instance, if you periodically spend $20 a week on Starbucks and need $80 a month to pay your light bill, a spending plan will clearly demonstrate that making your own coffee at home will get you the funds you need to cover that monthly electricity bill. Without a plan, you might just rationalize the coffee and say, "But it's only $20, and I absolutely love iced Passion Tango tea." A spending plan will show you what expenditures you can keep and what you'll need to eliminate immediately. At least for the meantime.

Although it isn't exactly fun to cut expenses, it certainly feels amazing when you have money to cover emergencies and everyday expenses, with more left over. So get disciplined and create that spending plan.

Don't delay. Sit down right now, and note how much money you have available (including savings), and then jot down all those necessary monthly expenses. Some examples of *necessary expenses* are:

- Shelter (rent or mortgage)
- Utilities
- Food
- Medications and Insurance Premiums and/or Copays
- Transportation (train or bus fare, auto payments and/or repairs, etc.)
- Education
- Child Care (include this if you have to put your kids in before-, after- or day care in order to make money)

- Other absolutely essential expenses (like parking fees after driving to work)

Once you have your list of necessities, you can figure out how much you have and how much you need. You can then use this list to eliminate all those things that you don't need to survive. For instance, if you're short on cash and need money to cover your rent/mortgage, you may have to eliminate dinners at restaurants (yes, even drive-throughs), plus the latest Apple or Droid gadget, Netflix, cable TV, unlimited text messaging, and even deodorant. OK, I'm just kidding about deodorant. Please keep deodorant on the necessity list.

Now take a really good look at your list again and then make additional cuts. How does your financial situation look now? Are you amazed that you had so much going out and not enough coming in? Were you able to cut back on wants to free up income for needs? Or did you realize that you still don't have enough money to cover bare necessities? Whatever your answer, I am proud of you for taking that first step to address the problem. Knowledge is power, and, now that you have this additional knowledge, you can improve your life right now.

So what happens if you don't have enough even after cutting expenses? Should you panic? Should you hide? Should you cry yourself to sleep and feel like a failure? Absolutely not. If you still don't have enough to make ends meet, it is time to get into planning mode. It is time to get creative, roll up those sleeves, and choose some proven moneymaking strategies and techniques.

Let's start with my recommended action plan.

Choose one of these plans of attack listed below on how to utilize the twenty-four sections herein which offer multiple ways to earn fast cash. Plan now. Act now. Start today.

- You can read my book in one setting, marking those opportunities that sound the best for you, and start **now** making each of them happen with a blitz-attack approach—filling out applications online, making phone calls to local businesses,

knocking on doors in your neighborhood—all while you await acceptance, callbacks, agreements from your neighbors.
- Commit to reading at least two numbered sections a day over the next fourteen days and choosing three options that day to implement immediately. Reassess daily, finding the best options for you and your current situation.
- More of a team player than a lone wolf? Enlist your spouse, your trusted friend fighting the same problems, various loyal and faithful family members. They may work with you on your chosen ways to earn fast money or they may be your alternate when you have scheduled two jobs that fall on the morning of the same day. Your spouse may choose to follow avenues which are not a good fit for you. Great! This doubles your family's chances of earning the emergency money you need and fast. The people in your life may just serve as accountability partners, to keep you motivated to try something new, to keep at this until you see the cash infusion you require. Just a note of caution here: choose wisely who you partner to work with, plus how you will handle the money distribution.
- Creatively choose your own path. If reading the ideas herein has birthed a new idea in you, or rekindled an old one, which your mind keeps thinking about, then check it out beforehand to confirm it's not some scam or to get the proper permits/licenses you may need, and go for it!

Regardless of which plan you implement, you must follow up with repeated actions. So decide and move forward. Don't give up!

And, for those of you who have enough, it's now time to earn more so that you can prepare for future emergencies and build strong wealth. Are you ready? I hope so. Let's get started.

#1: Unclaimed Property

Before we delve into how to make more money, the good news is that you may already have money coming to you that you can claim. Unclaimed property consists of funds or items that may be owed to you, whether by the government, banks, credit unions, pensions, and other sources. It includes stocks, funds in checking and savings accounts, trust distributions, unredeemed money orders, gift certificates, payroll checks, insurance payments, refunds, and other property. Interestingly, millions of dollars' worth of unclaimed property is sitting and waiting for its owners to make a claim each year. To determine if you have any unclaimed property, you'll simply need to input qualifying information into databases to discover if any await you.

So gather your social security number, any variations of your name (nicknames; previous surnames and/or current, married, and maiden names; misspelled versions), your middle initials and/or middle name, and your current and past addresses. Once you have this information, you can then conduct online searches to determine if unclaimed property awaits you.

Here are a few sites to check out for unclaimed property in your name:

National Association of Unclaimed Property Administration

The National Association of Unclaimed Property Administrators (NAUPA) site allows you to search using your name(s) in each of the fifty states. Companies must send funds from "lost" accounts to the state of the last known address for the account holder. If you do a search and find that you have unclaimed property, you should fill out a claim, provided on the site, to get the process started.

Check out its website here: https://www.unclaimed.org/

The Missing Money website is endorsed and sponsored by NAUPA and offers free multistate searches for unclaimed properties. Unclaimed properties include stocks, bonds, dividends, mutual funds, insurance policies, trust funds, escrow accounts, wages and uncashed checks, safety deposit box contents and bank accounts, CDs, and utility deposits.

In most cases, claims can be made in perpetuity or indefinitely, although places, like California, are trying to lay claim to these funds after they have been declared abandoned for government use. Fortunately it's very easy to find out if you have unclaimed funds.

1. The first step would be to write down all the states where you may have opened an account or have a close relative who may have left you money.
2. Visit the NAUPA website and do a search for all these states by typing in your name. For each search, you may have to do at least two searches if female: one with your maiden name and one with your married name (or any previously married names).
3. If you get a hit, you may file for a claim. The property, if deemed abandoned, will have been converted to cash and turned over to the appropriate state for safekeeping. You can only claim on the principal amount, not the accrued interest or any other earnings the fund may have accumulated. For property to be declared abandoned, it must stay dormant or untouched for at least three to seven years.

Check out its website here: http://www.missingmoney.com/

But don't just stop there. You can try your individual state treasury offices as well. For instance, Illinois residents can visit https://icash.illinoistreasurer.gov/, New York residents can visit http://www.osc.state.ny.us/ouf/, California residents can visit https://ucpi.sco.ca.gov/UCP/, and residents in other states can also search for their local state controller or treasurer's office.

US Department of Veterans Affairs

The US Department of Veterans Affairs has an unclaimed fund website that allows you to search for unclaimed property if you're a current or former policy holder or beneficiary. To search here, you should have the veteran's first and last name. If you find money is owed to that person, you should contact the US Department of Veterans Affairs' office to give them further identifying information to ensure the money is yours before it is released to you.

Check out its website here: https://insurance.va.gov/UnclaimedFunds

Internal Revenue Service

You may also have money unclaimed or undelivered by the Internal Revenue Service (IRS). If you had earned an income, but you did not file a return (due to your earnings falling below the IRS filing requirement), then you may have some money owed to you. To collect money from such tax returns you were not legally required to file, you must file one now with the IRS within three years of not being required to file said return. There is no penalty for filing late returns under this scenario. If your check was not deliverable, it would then have been returned to the IRS. You can visit their website, or call 800-829-3676, where a representative should be able to tell you if the IRS has any unclaimed funds for you.

Check out its website here: https://www.irs.gov/uac/does-the-irs-have-money-waiting-for-you

United States Department of Labor

Check out the United States Department of Labor's website. With this site, you'll search using your various employers' names. Your wages are held for three years; after that time, the money is sent to the US Treasury for safekeeping. If you do find that you are owed back wages, you must send a claim form to the Wage and Hour Division.

Check out its website here: http://webapps.dol.gov/wow/

The Federal Deposit Insurance Corporation

The Federal Deposit Insurance Corporation (FDIC) has an unclaimed search option for those who may have had money in an institution that failed. The FDIC acquires the funds after the financial institution is closed. If you do a search and find that you may be owned funds, you should print and fill out the FDIC Claimant Verification form and have it notarized. Then mail it in and wait to be contacted within thirty days. Knowing this could be a month long wait, you must be working other emergency funding avenues in the meantime to reach the fourteen-day deadline.

Check out its website here: https://www5.fdic.gov/funds/index.asp

The Social Security Administration

The Social Security Administration also has over 220 million accounts and $250 billion in unclaimed funds. More than an estimated $499 million dollars in benefit payments are not cashed each year. There is no time limit to request reissuance of a check.

Check out its website here: https://www.ssa.gov/

Treasury Direct

Treasury Direct has a search feature called Treasury Hunt, their search tool to see if savings bonds or registered Treasury Notes have matured and are no longer earning interest. The system has information on Series E bonds issued after 1974, which have reached full maturity. If you search and find that you are missing a bond, you should file a claim by submitting FS Form 1048. The form can be downloaded or sent to you through the mail.

Check out its website here:
https://www.treasurydirect.gov/indiv/tools/tools_treasuryhunt.htm

Pension Benefit Guaranty Corporation

Pension Benefit Guaranty Corporation (PBGC) is another site to check out. According to the NAUPA (the National Association of Unclaimed Property Administrators), $58 billion remains in unclaimed funds. This fund comes from unclaimed payroll or inheritance checks, returned checks, unclaimed insurance payments, abandoned bank accounts, lost savings bonds, old 401(k)s, unclaimed pensions, utilities' security deposits, and dividends. About $300 million of these unclaimed funds are with the PBGC, given to that agency after a company closes its retirement plan or its operations.

More than forty million private American workers are covered by PBGC. This agency was created by the 1974 Employee Retirement Income Security Act (ERISA) to protect retirement pension plans and ensure affordable pension insurance premiums for voluntary private pension plans.

You can use the PBGC database to search for unclaimed pension benefits. As of 2015, the PBGC lists more than 38,000 cases of unclaimed payments with amounts ranging from a few cents to close to one million dollars. The PBGC says the average unclaimed amount is $9,100! If you have any reason to believe that you have funds with PBGC, the steps are relatively simple to process payment.

1. Download the forms from the PBGC website and submit online. You should retain your own copies of the form.
2. Organize your supporting documents (pay slips, W-2 forms).
3. Check for spousal payments.
4. Get vested in a pension plan because benefits are usually electronically deposited into your account as a direct deposit.

Check out its website here: http://search.pbgc.gov/mp/mp.aspx

The National Registry of Unclaimed Retirement Benefits

The National Registry of Unclaimed Retirement Benefits is a nonprofit subsidiary of PenChecks Inc. This corporation is a processor of retirement benefits and helps former workers find their unclaimed benefits with the website's extensive free-to-use database culled from national PenChecks transactions. The database is updated regularly and has partnered with other organizations to ensure the best coverage of unclaimed retirement benefits.

To find out if you have any unclaimed retirement benefits from PenChecks Inc., please do the following:

1. Input your Social Security number in the space provided on their website's database.
2. If you find your name (or that of a loved one), provide the registry with your contact details so that payout arrangements may be made by your employer.
3. The registry will be responsible for contacting your employer via email to give them your contact details and to inform them that you want to get paid. The responsibility of your employer, once that notice email is received, is to send you the benefits forms to fill out so instructions can be properly set forth regarding payment of your benefits.

Check out its website here:
https://www.unclaimedretirementbenefits.com/

MIB Group, Inc.

MIB Group, Inc., previously called Medical Information Bureau, is a nonprofit, member-owned group offering underwriting services under the banner of full disclosure that alerts its members from the United States and Canada of any errors on insurance applications. They also offer Cross Check, a confidential search for unclaimed property for relatives of deceased policyholders. Cross Check cross-references specific data, like Social Security numbers and dates of birth against more than three thousand private and public death notices, among other sources.

The MIB offers a service that could prove very useful for the millions of Americans unaware that they are beneficiaries of a property, like a life insurance policy. Earlier this year, CBS reported that insurance companies are not always diligent in trying to find the beneficiaries of deceased clients. Insurance companies are required to submit a report of unclaimed property and transfer said amount after it becomes dormant to the appropriate state treasurer. With Cross Check, individuals don't have to wait for the funds to be transferred to the state treasurer before they begin searching for unclaimed property.

To use the MIB Consumer File database, you must first be a member of any of their member companies. This means you must have an active individual (not group) insurance plan within the last seven years. Finally the free search is only valid once a year.

Check out its website here: http://www.mib.com/lost_life_insurance.html

If you're owed money as a descendant …

After you've search for unclaimed property in your name, you might want to see if you're owed money as a descendant. A lot of unclaimed money belongs to descendants, and someone may have left you some funds. You must meet many requirements to qualify for benefits as a descendant. For instance, you may qualify if you're the spouse (living in the same house as the descendant at the time of the descendant's death), or the child or parent of the descendant, who was on the descendant's record for at least one month before the death, etc. For a complete list of qualifications, www.ssa.gov/form/ssa-1724.html.

Once you've determined that you're qualified to receive benefits, you can conduct a search using the deceased's first and last name, social security number (if known), state where the money would be issued (if known), state where the death occurred, plus year of birth and year of death. You will also need to provide your name, email address, and physical address. There is no charge for this service. To have the results sent to you by email, the charge is $18. To have the information sent to you via First Class mail, the charge is $22.

Check out its website here: https://www.ssa.gov/forms/ssa-1724.html

Additional Tips:

Keep in mind that databases are often incomplete, and, although organizations and government entities do their best to update information, the system may say that you have no lost money when you do. Therefore, don't be afraid to make written requests for your cash. After all, you may very well have money although it's listed that you don't.

Contact any state you previously lived in to see if you can recover any lost funds. Oftentimes companies will simply send the funds to their home state if they can't locate you via your past address.

Contact any people, companies, organizations, or corporations where you were required to pay deposits. For instance, if you initially had average or not-so-good credit, you may have been asked for a security deposit by your utility company or landlord. If you have now established a good reputation of paying your rent or utilities on time, you may get that security deposit back. By the same token, you may have uncashed bonus or overtime checks, lost insurance refunds, and the like.

You may be the beneficiary to a life insurance policy that you're unaware of and thus entitled to the deceased person's policy proceeds. Therefore, if you think you're the beneficiary and have legal rights to search the deceased person's effects, then you go through the deceased person's mail, any insurance policy loan interest payouts, income tax returns, safety deposit boxes, personal documents, or check the deceased person's employers, membership organizations, etc. Note: It's advised that you seek legal representation before pursuing this action.

#2: About Those Annoying Creditors: Contact Them Now!

Hopefully you found some unclaimed property. If not, don't worry. There are many remaining options to help you get the money you need. Now, before we delve into them, it's important that you let your creditors know about your financial situation. Contact them right now and update them, preferably before they call and threaten you.

Contacting them may feel like you're admitting defeat, but you're not. By taking the initiative, you are seizing control of the situation and demonstrating that you are responsible. You're showing by your actions that you want to make things right and are willing to do whatever you can to clear your debt.

When you call your creditors, explain your financial situation to the representative. Inform them that you want to pay the funds but are unable to do so at this time. Tell them the truth: that you've lost your job, had an unforeseen medical emergency, whatever. Let them know that you don't yet have the funds to cover your bills but explain that you are working on an action plan right now and will have the funds soon.

If you get someone who refuses to help or treats you disrespectfully, thank them for their time and then call back and speak to someone else. Don't give up asking for assistance until you find someone who is willing or able to assist you. It may take several times to reach someone helpful but don't give up until you do.

Be sure to note their name, plus the date and time of your call, the phone number you dialed, and the agreement reached between the two of you. You may need this information later.

A simple phone call, with the right person, can help you avoid late fees, legal action, and even annoying telephone calls. Communicating openly about your situation can also help you negotiate a payoff plan and keep your credit score from plummeting. It can also give you a little bit of breathing room. For instance, the representative may offer you lower payments or the opportunity to postpone them for a set time. With a mortgage, you may be offered a mortgage modification. One note of caution here. Some mortgage "modifications" may be noted as "foreclosures" which would not help your credit rating. Be sure to ask about this specifically with your mortgage representative and get your answer in writing. With student loans, you may be eligible for a deferment (where interest is not capitalized or paid by government) or a forbearance (where interest accrues).

Either way, the sooner you contact your creditors, the more options you'll have and hopefully the less stressed you'll feel.

Check out Government and Private Programs for Utilities

After you contact your creditors, it is now time to inquire about government and private programs that may help you pay your utilities. You see, many utility companies—as well as charities, and federal and state government organizations—offer assistance programs. Many of these organizations may have emergency grants available to pay all or a portion of your utility bill when you don't have the funds to do so.

With this in mind, you'll need to contact your utility companies and ask about any programs they offer. Many times their programs aren't advertised but are available for long-term customers. At the very least, many utility companies will offer payment plans that will allow you to pay a fixed amount each month that could help out in a pinch. Here are a few you can check out!

Duke Energy (South Carolina, North Carolina, and Florida)

Duke Energy is an electric power company operating in South Carolina, North Carolina, and Florida. They have over 7.3 million customers and, in 2011, merged with Progress Energy. Last year they decided to acquire a natural gas company, Piedmont Natural Gas—a deal expected to be finalized by the end of 2016.

The company has low-income finance assistance programs, but you need to contact their Customer Service office at 800-700-8744 or 800-

943-6914 to find out more about their payment arrangements. Essentially you can request extra time to pay your bills or inquire about a lower rate. This company has a very strict policy regarding late payments or bounced checks for people in their payment assistance programs. So always get the correct information of where to send the payments and get the full name of the person you made the arrangements with. If you happen to be late in paying or your check bounced, they do have a reputation for adding late charges and/or slapping on a new deposit charge. Therefore, be very diligent about making those arranged payments on time and for the correct amount.

In addition to the above payment plans, they also offer some noteworthy programs. They are as follows:

Share the Warmth (Carolina Residents)

The Share the Warmth program was established in 1985 to help Carolina residents with their winter heating bills. The program is funded by customers, the Duke Energy Foundation, and its employees. The program provides assistance with heating bills during the winter season to those who meet income-eligibility requirements.

Cooling Assistance (Carolina Residents)

The Cooling Assistance program assists individuals and families that need help paying for their energy costs associated with the extreme temperatures during the summer in the Carolinas. The heat can be dangerous for many people, especially those with health problems and the elderly.

Fan-Heat Relief (Carolina Residents)

The Fan-Heat Relief program helps senior citizens in the Carolinas to have some sort of cooling in their homes during the summer. The program is administered by the NC Department of Human Resources, Division of Aging. The funds are distributed beginning in May.

Energy Neighbor Fund (Florida Residents)

The Energy Neighbor Fund program is for Duke Energy's Florida customers and Duke Energy Progress customers. The program helps eligible individuals and families pay their home energy bill regardless of what kind of heating source they have. Eligibility is determined by the Energy Neighbor Fund partner agencies. The program has been able to help thousands of households since it began.

Helping Hand (Indiana Residents)

Helping Hand provides assistance during the winter to Indiana customers. The program was established in 1983 and is funded by shareholders, employees, and Duke Energy customers. Needy customers who meet a certain criteria will be given a one-time payment of $300 credited to their account. To be eligible, you must be a residential customer and meet their income guidelines.

WinterCare (Kentucky Residents)

The WinterCare program assists customers who are Kentucky residents with their winter heating bills. If the customer is eligible for this program, a one-time payment will be made to their account as long as these funds are available. Please contact the Northern Kentucky Community Action Commission at 859.581.6607 for more information.

HeatShare (Ohio Residents)

The HeatShare program assists Ohio residents with their winter heating bills. Established in 1986, HeatShare is administered by the Salvation Army with eligibility based upon need and the customer's receipt of a disconnection notice. The program starts in mid-January and runs through April 30 or until these funds run out. For more information, contact the Salvation Army at 513-762-5636 after the program begins.

For more information about these programs, please visit https://www.duke-energy.com/community/customer%20assistance%20programs

Florida Power & Light

Florida Power & Light is the one of the largest electric utility companies in the country with over 4.8 million customers. They also have programs in place to help those unable to meet payment deadlines such as:

Payment extension: Depending on your account history with the company, you can get an extension on your due date. However, you will incur late payment charges of 1.5% on the balance or $5, whichever is higher.

FEMA Emergency Food Shelter (FEMAEFSP): If FEMA has available funds, it can give financial assistance to low-income families, like one month's utility payment; one month's rent, food, and minor home repairs.

Elderly Home Energy Assistance Program (EHEAP): Available to low-income families with at least one person living in the home aged sixty or older. The financial assistance can only be given twice a year (October through March and April through September).

Check out its website here: https://www.fpl.com/save/pdf/financial-assistance.pdf

American States Water Company

Servicing customers in California, American States Water Company operates through the Golden State Water Company and American States Utility Services. The key to preventing disconnection of services is to inform the company beforehand that you cannot pay on time. You can reach Golden State at 1-800-999-4033. The company allows you to pay in small increments but you must not miss a payment or your service will be disconnected. Also, under the California Alternate Rates for Water, you can qualify for a monthly discount of $8 if you fall within the low-income profile.

Although countless nonprofit agencies and charities offer emergency financial help, here are a few well-known ones:

Low-Income Home Energy Assistance Program Block Grant

This LIHEAP grant is funded by the Federal Department of Health and Human Services (DHHS). They provide two types of services. The first is for low-income individuals who may receive financial assistance to offset the cost of heating or cooling their homes or to have their home weatherized to make it more energy efficient. Applications are usually taken at community action agencies. These agencies will also have additional information on many other resources in your area.

LIHEAP crisis programs are available to low-income families who are faced with a disconnection or if they are low on heating fuel or oil. The funds will be sent directly to the utility company. This program is available in the winter and summer months. To qualify for this program you must meet some or all of these requirements:

- The applicant has been threatened with a disconnection of their heating or other utility or
- Must have their heating or utility service disconnected or
- Must have less than a ten-day supply of heating oil, kerosene, propane, or wood or
- Must have broken, inoperable, or unsafe heating equipment.

For additional information, please visit http://liheap.org/

Lifeline (Universal Service Fund of the Federal Communications Commission Office)

The government has a benefit program called Lifeline that operates under the Universal Service Fund of the Federal Communications Commission office. The fund can be used to help citizens pay for their phone service, provided they fall under a certain income level.

There are similar programs for energy bills (LIHEAP), medical care and maintenance drugs, emergency medical treatment (EMTALA), and welfare (TANF) that covers food, housing, and other expenses.

To utilize these services, you need to approach the respective local agency in your state and apply. The eligibility rules mainly are concerned with your circumstances and income level. There are two ways to qualify: low-income or program-based. Once you are approved, this qualification is only valid for one year, and you must get reapproved if you want financial assistance for the next year.

Visit http://www.needhelppayingbills.com for more information on how to access their bill-payment process and the list of banks that they have enlisted to assist them.

Here are some other organizations to help you with paying your bills:

Salvation Army

There should be a local Salvation Army in your area. This organization offers help to families and individuals so their utilities are not cut off suddenly. Under their HeatShare program and Gas Affordability program, one must qualify first before the Salvation Army can step in and help pay your bill. You can call their hotline at 1-800-842-7279 if you are from the Minnesota area or your local Salvation Army office.

Here is their website link: http://salvationarmynorth.org/programs-that-help/basic-needs/heatshare/

Temporary Assistance for Needy Families (TANF)

Every state has a TANF office. This is a short-term welfare-assistance package for families who cannot afford to pay for their rent, electricity, food, job training, child care, and other necessary daily expenses.

Each state has its own operations manual and benefits eligibility criteria.

Tenant-Based Rental Assistance (TBRA)

This is financial assistance to help individual families pay for their rent. It is unlike other HOME Investment Partnership programs in that a family can move to a different residence and still be eligible for rent assistance, and the subsidy will be based on the income of the family rather than a standard assistance plan.

Project-Based Rental Assistance (PBRA)

Under a law passed in 1974, the PBRA—which is part of the HUD—was given a $2 billion fund to help with rental subsidies for those living in cooperative apartment projects and other government housing projects. However, the individuals or families must meet the eligibility requirements, such as income level.

In addition, under the law, only 25% of those living in these projects can qualify to get the rent subsidy voucher, not including the sick, elderly, or disabled.

Community Service Block Grant (CSBG)

The objectives of the CSBG include:

- Decreasing the number of homeless individuals and

- Helping migrants and low-income individuals meet their daily needs, including housing, nutrition, health, living conditions, and the presence of a support system.

The CSBG not only helps with rent and payment of utilities, they can also provide assistance with education, employment, emergency services, and food, among others. They adopted the LIHEAP program to help them manage their assistance operations.

Gradient Gives Back Foundation

Based in Minnesota, the Gradient Gives Back Foundation is a nonprofit group that aims to help underprivileged and distressed American families. Eligible families are given one year of mortgage or rental payments from funds raised through their partner charities.

United Way 2-1-1

This is a global organization that helps build communities and strengthen families through financial and other forms of assistance. The 2-1-1 in their corporate name is a telephone number that Americans can call when they need help with health and human services. The organization also offers free tax preparation, assistance for parents with children in school, and the Play60 program, which makes sure that children have access to exercise and nutritious food.

Housing Finance Agencies

There is an HFA office in every state, and they are tasked with helping American families find affordable housing. They have three federal programs:

1. Housing Bond
2. Housing Credit
3. HOME or Home Investment Partnerships

They help with mortgage payments and also assist low-income families buy their first home or rent their first apartment.

USA Cares

USA Cares is a nonprofit charitable organization with over 84,000 clients. They have been able to save over 3,500 homes from financial distress and are very diligent in screening applicants eligible for their financial assistance programs.

Aside from their housing assistance, they also help with employment, emergency services, and military men and women injured in combat.

Joe-4-Oil Heating Program

This program offers heating assistance to low-income families or families under distress. They operate under the Citizens Energy group and give free heating oil to deserving families in twenty-five states. Eligible families get a one-time delivery of one hundred gallons of heating oil.

To apply, call their number at 1-877-JOE-4-OIL. There is no online application, but the forms to be filled out will be mailed to you.

Jewish Federation of Greater Los Angeles

This organization, based in Los Angeles, is determined to help any Jew in need. They have several programs, such as Emerging from Poverty to Self Sufficiency, Frail Seniors, Holocaust Survivors, Disabled Jews, and those affected by domestic violence, divorce, and addiction.

For financial assistance, they have about eight partners who can help with college funding, scholarships, financial crises, and loans.

Federal Trade Commission

The Federal Trade Commission can help you with your credit card debt through their debt settlement program, problems with collectors, or finding some relief from your tax payments.

They can help you plan a payment schedule that is manageable and legal. They can also help lower the balance due through a compromise or installment agreement.

American Credit Counseling Service

Founded in 1988, the ACCS is a nonprofit organization that offers free guidance and consultation on budgeting, money management, and solutions to lowering debt.

The ACCS is proud to help everyone who applies, and they do not screen or turn away people.

InCharge Debt Solutions

This nonprofit organization offers debt relief solutions to those with unmanageable credit card or other debt. One call and you get a credit counselor to help you with your situation. The analysis given to you will be completely objective without proposing a new loan to cover your debt.

Often they propose debt consolidation or counseling on housing issues, student loans, and bankruptcy.

MilitaryOneSource.mil

Military personnel can turn to this organization for financial assistance. The site helps with almost all matters pertaining to personal finances, including housing, taxes, education, health, special needs, relocation, casualty assistance, travel, recreation, and disaster recovery.

They also have one-time financial relief for rent, utilities, funeral expenses, repairs, and medical expenses. To get started on the road to financial recovery and stability, call 800-342-9647 for a free consultation.

#3: Loans

Bank Loans

Although grants are typically the first choice (since you don't have to pay back those funds), there may come a time when you need to borrow money to cover your expenses.

Banks have been known to offer loans to borrowers who have very good credit and/or high income, which does not really benefit those who have lower incomes. To address this discrepancy, some banks produced a program, sponsored by the FDIC, that offers lower-interest-rate bank loans (15%) to individuals who have lower income. The program is called the FDIC Small-Dollar Loan Pilot Program. The rates are far lower than using other options, such as payday loans or other high-risk, high-interest options. Thirty-one banks offer the program, and that number will likely increase.

Here are some sites you can check out for more information about the FDIC's Small-Dollar Loan Pilot Program:

Amarillo National Bank

https://www.anb.com/amarillo-economy.aspx

First State Bank

https://fsb.bank/business/borrow/small-business-administration-sba-loans

National Bank of KC

https://www.nbkc.com/personal/loans/small_dollar_loans.aspx

Oklahoma State Bank

http://www.osbbank.com/business-loans

Heritage Bank

http://www.heritagebanknw.com/home/business/loans/sba

For additional banks participating in the program, please visit https://www.fdic.gov/bank/analytical/quarterly/...3/2008_Quarterly_Vol2No3.html

Government Loans

Govloans.gov

If you are looking for a loan for disaster relief or housing, then you should contact Govloans. Under disaster relief, you may be eligible for a government loan if you are a victim of a natural phenomenon and your area has been declared to be a disaster area. However, not everyone can avail of this loan as there are requirements such as:

- Your ability to repay the loan;
- Your property sustained physical damage;
- Your business was affected.

Under the Housing section of this website are several types of loans, like the Property Improvement loan, which is available to property owners, persons in the process of buying a property under an installment plan, and lessees with at least a six-month lease contract.

If you would like more information or to inquire about interest rates, call 1 (800) 333-4636.

Business and Personal Loans

In addition to government based-loans, you can also apply for two other types of loans: business or personal. You can obtain these via a bank, credit union, or even a peer-to-peer (P2P) lending organization. One benefit of using a P2P institution is that you can borrow money based mainly on a credit check and debt-to-income ratio.

If you have a credit letter grade of AA, you can get a higher loan amount. The most popular websites for P2P are LendingClub.com and Prosper.com and a new site generating a lot of interest—Kabbage.com—which has been approving loans quickly and sending the money electronically through PayPal.

P2P lending has grown over the past years with the introduction of crowdfunding, and this has helped refined the concept and protect both lenders and borrowers alike. The main difference between P2P lending and crowdfunding (although they are similar in a number of ways) is in the way the funds are generated. With P2P, the company decides and approves the loan as a direct funding with interest usually payable in three to five years; whereas, with crowdfunding, the people decide. If your story strikes a chord with investors, they may just invest in you and your cause.

Crowdfunding investors have two options: shares in your business or rewards/prizes in exchange for their donation. The downside of crowdfunding is that, if you don't raise 100% of the amount requested, you don't get access to the funds at all. Plus not all crowdfunding investors are interested in making money from their donations. Some investors just want repayment when your business gets off the ground.

Another popular crowdfunding website is Kickstarter.com, which has approved over 7,500 projects or a little under half of the requests filed.

Other crowdfunding sites are Kickfurther.com, Kiva.com, and IndieGoGo.com. Here's a bit of information about each of these:

Kickfurther

Kickfurther is a crowdfunding website that helps businesses get the funding they need. When a company is formed, the owners sometimes underestimate how much money will be needed to continue production of their product. This is where Kickfurther comes in. Companies complete an ad that describes their product and then users can decide if they wish to contribute money to those products. The amount of money needed will vary from company to company. The average return for those that do contribute is 22%. It is important to remember that risks are involved when contributing money to these companies. If the company fails to deliver its products, Kickfurther will liquidate the products, which means you will have a smaller return on your money.

Check out its website here: https://www.kickfurther.com

Kiva

Kiva is a person-to-person microlending website that operates all over the world. To be eligible for a loan, you need to have a legitimate business, not involved in illegal activity and has not filed for bankruptcy. The loan must be used for business purposes only. The maximum amount a business can borrow is $10,000 with an interest rate of 0%. Interested individuals can go to the website and decide what businesses they would like to contribute money to. The loans given on this site have a 97% repayment rate. However, Kiva does not guarantee repayment for any of the loans granted on their website. If a company defaults on its loan, the loaner will receive an email and should consider the remaining balance due as a loss.

Check out its website here: https://www.kiva.org

Indiegogo

The Indiegogo crowdfunding website offers both fixed and flexible funding. The site also provides a platform that allows companies to sell the finished products when they are ready. People can visit the website and look at the different campaigns and decide which of them to contribute their money to. If you have contributed money to a campaign, you can request a refund as long as the campaign is still in progress. However, you are not able to get a refund if the money has already been transferred to the campaign owner, if the campaign has ended, if the term of the campaign has been fulfilled, or if the campaign was deemed to be against Indiegogo's terms of service.

Check out its website here: https://www.indiegogo.com

What You Need to Know about the P2P Loan Process

- Approval and release of funds can happen in one week;
- Loan terms are flexible from three months to five years;
- Rate of interest varies and is usually higher than bank rates;
- There are usually no early repayment fees;
- There are arrangement fees to be paid, sometimes upfront.

Quick Facts about Crowdfunding

- Women tend to have a higher success rate in raising crowdfunding than men with a 71%:61% women-to-men success ratio.
- Compelling stories get funding and always answer the question "Why?"
- Build a strong network before you start a crowdfunding project.
- Research the project's potential fully before launching.
- If you can name backers or prominent and respected individuals who endorse your project, you have a higher chance of getting more individuals involved.

GoFundMe

Another way to seek emergency funds is to set up a GoFundMe page. This platform makes it easy to raise money during an emergency money crisis. The company was founded in 2010 and is based in San Diego, California. This site enables individuals to personalize fund-raising campaigns and share it on social media. GoFundMe does deduct a 5% fee from each donation and a processing fee of 3%. Then all the money collected goes directly to the person requesting the funds.

You can make a fund-raising campaign for yourself, a friend, or a loved one. It can include things such as help with medical payments, volunteer programs, education costs, funerals, memorials, and even pet medical expenses. You can make a fund-raising campaign for almost anything as long as it is not illegal and does not contain any inappropriate content, like ammunition, illegal drugs, illegal investments, etc. For a complete list of illegal or inappropriate offerings, please visit https://www.gofundme.com/terms.

To get started, create your GoFundMe account. You can sign up using either your email address or a link your Facebook account. (Linking your account with Facebook will make it easier to share your funding request via social media.) You will then be taken to a page where you enter the amount of money you would like to raise in your campaign and will be asked to enter a title for your campaign. After this you should select a picture and write a small description that includes:

- Who you are;
- Who (or what) you need the money for;
- How the money will be used;
- How fast you need the money to cover costs;
- Why you think you should receive the money;
- What sets you apart from others asking for money;
- How thankful you will be to receive the cash;
- Any other pertinent information to demonstrate need, trust, and sincerity.

After you have set up your campaign, share your campaign site with family and friends, plus also invite email contacts, and post to social media sites to gain attention. The more people who see your campaign, the better your chances that someone will donate money to your campaign. There is no limit to the amount of time your campaign can stay active. Many keep their campaigns active even after reaching their goals. You can post updates to your campaign and send thank-you notes to those who have donated.

All donations made through the site are completely secure, and you, the requester of funds, can withdraw your money whenever you want. You do not need to wait until you reach your goal to request money from your campaign. You should provide GoFundMe with your bank account information, and it will take five to seven business days for the money to be deposited into your account.

Unemployment Insurance

Besides the P2P funding possibilities listed in the previous section, other options are available if you need funds quickly. For instance, you might qualify for unemployment insurance (UI) if you find yourself in a predicament where you have been fired from your job, at no fault of your own. One benefit of this type of insurance is that it can act as a lifeline until you can find employment. These benefits come from the Department of Labor and will pay minimal amounts to help you with your basic needs.

The premise for approval of UI is that the individual is not working but is actively trying to find suitable employment. To get approved for UI, the individual must:

- Have worked long enough to earn UI wages to cover the base unemployment period,
- Be physically fit and able to work,
- Be available to work and ready to work,
- Have been looking for a job and has not stopped applying for jobs.

This individual can also apply for training benefits but must first seek approval with the local Department of Labor.

There is usually also a phone interview and a waiting period as the state DOL employee verifies the information provided and checks your work records. Benefits, once approved, are given weekly. If not approved, the individual can file an appeal.

Recently a private UI firm was launched, called IncomeAssure. If you lose your job, you could get half of your pretax weekly salary up to $250,000 in annual income only. If you are not approved for state UI, this company will increase the benefits to cover what is not paid for by the state for a maximum of twenty-four weeks.

For more information about this program, please visit https://www.incomeassure.com/.

Payday Loans/Salary Advances

Payday loans have always been known as a popular go-to source for a quick bailout when your finances are running a little short. However, these types of short-term loans are known to be quite expensive in the long run.

With a payday loan, you will write a personal check payable to the payday loan company for the amount you wish to borrow plus the fee that they charge for their service. They will hold the check until the loan is due, which is usually your next payday. The amount of the fees can be a percentage of the amount you borrow or it can be based on increments of the money borrowed. The company must tell you what the total cost of the loan will be.

For example, if you want to borrow $100 and the fee is $15, you will write a check for $115. If you want to rollover the loan, you will be charged another $15 loan fee. The annual percentage rate can be as high as 391%, and the loans usually become due in fifteen to ninety days.

Here are a few tips before you decide to borrow money from a payday company:

- Choose a lender tied to larger institutions instead of a fly-by-night standalone company.
- Find a company that is up front about their loan requirements.
- Look at the company's interest rate and any fees, especially for prepayment, and make sure the company is transparent about any interest rates.
- Ensure that you have the right documentation to get approved for a loan.
- Make sure you understand the terms and conditions of the loan process and any repayment procedures.

Salary Advance Loans

The terms of a salary advance will depend on the employer. Some charge for pushing through the additional paperwork, while others don't charge anything at all. However, all salary advances must be repaid on a set schedule. The repayment terms are usually slated for the next pay date (being automatically deducted from your standard paycheck amount) or to be repaid on a mutually agreed-upon schedule, such as 25% every payday until repaid in full.

However, Salary Advance Loans were created by Credit Unions (SECU) as a better alternative. Loan amounts run between $50–$500, with an interest rate of 18%. Repayment is normally due in thirty days. These loans are designed to advance a portion of your paycheck for your immediate use.

To apply for a salary advance loan, you must be a member of the credit union or know someone who is a member who is also willing to endorse you. If you're not, you'll be required to open a special advance-cash account with the credit union you are trying to borrow money from. Typically you should make a 5% deposit (based on the funds you wish to borrow) to open your account. In addition, a percentage of the total salary loan must remain on deposit in the account, which is eligible for dividends. Once this deposited amount reaches the loan amount, yet the loan is not due, the loan interest rate may drop to 5.5%.

If you are seeking to borrow more than $500, you may need to make a bigger deposit. You may also be required to have your paycheck deposited into the credit union account. Most of the time, the loan is due on your next payday. The amount of money you can borrow is usually one-third of what your take-home pay is.

Almost all credit unions offer these types of loans.

Mortgage Modification Loans

Homeowners who are facing a financial emergency that could lead to the foreclosure of their home may want to work with their lender to get a loan modification loan. Sometimes these loans are called a workout plan or a mortgage modification or restructuring. Doing this will change the terms of the mortgage so that the homeowner can afford the mortgage payment.

The Home Affordable Modification Program (HAMP) was created by the government in 2009 and is part of the Making Home Affordable Program designed to help provide financial relief for homeowners facing financial emergencies. It will give you a lower interest rate, extend the term of the loan, and lower the loan principle.

To qualify for the program:

- You must have had your mortgage before January 1, 2009;
- The home must be your primary residence;
- You must owe no more than $729,750 on a single-family unit; up to $934,200 on a two-unit rental property; $1,129,250 on a three-unit rental property; or $1,403,400 on a four-unit rental property.
- The property must not have been condemned;
- You must have enough documented income to prove that you can pay the new monthly principle and interest amount as per your loan modification;
- You must have a financial hardship such as loss in income, divorce, or illness (you should prove the hardship with documentation and sign an affidavit).

You should provide some or all of the following documents:

- Tax returns;
- Recent pay stubs;
- Credit card statements;
- A list of assets and their estimated values;
- A letter detailing your dire financial situation;
- Loan statements.

Check out its website here:
https://www.treasury.gov/initiatives/financial-stability/TARP-Programs/housing/mha/Pages/hamp.aspx

Cal Vet Modification

If you have a VA loan, a special government program called the Cal Vet Modification helps those who need a loan modification. Those with an FHA loan should go through the loan modification program specifically for Federal Housing Administration loans.

Once you have gathered all the information required by the lender, you can call the lender to get the loan modification started. Make sure that you have all the required documentation so that your file does not get pushed to the bottom of the pile because something was missing. You do not have to be delinquent on your monthly payments to obtain a loan modification. However, you should show that you are likely to default on your loan payments if a loan modification does not take place. If you are not comfortable talking to the lender, you may want to consider seeking an attorney or contacting your local HUD-approved counseling agency. If you are facing foreclosure on the property, applying for a loan modification will place a temporary halt on the foreclosure process. Having a loan modification done should not impact your credit score greatly. The loan modifications are reported in a way that it should not currently harm your credit score. A mortgage is considered sustainable if the monthly payment is 31% of the monthly gross income.

Make sure to stay in touch with the modification lender. Call them at least once a week to check on the progress of your loan modification. Ask them if your file documentation is complete or if you need to submit any additional information. If so, gather it as quickly as possible and send it in. The faster you provide the documentation that the lender requires, the faster the loan modification process goes. If your situation has changed since you sent in your packet and documentation, let the lender know right away. These changes could be a new job and/or a reduction in the amount of monthly gross income you have coming in.

Check out its website here: https://www.calvet.ca.gov/HomeLoans

#4: Selling Stuff

Now that we've discussed many creative ways you can make ends meet with unclaimed property, grants, loans, and more, we will now discuss how you can make emergency money using your skills and qualifications. These methods will require a bit of action, but, if you willing to put forth the effort, you will surely reap the benefits. We'll start with selling stuff ... all kinds of stuff.

Emergency Money by Selling Cell Phones for Cash

Selling your unused cell phones is one way to make a quick buck, and it's done all the time—online and off-line. However, before you start marketing your old phones, you should do some basic preparations to ensure that you get a good price and to protect your privacy.

First, remove data to protect your privacy. This task cannot be overemphasized. According to Venture Beat, mobile phones carry six potential security threats. These are:

- Potential for the phone itself to be used for terrorist acts,
- Hacking of the phone's data to find payment and bank details,
- Tracking online movements of the previous owners via GPS,
- Eavesdropping on others' telephone conversations in the nearby area or hijacking of Internet services/transactions also in the nearby area,
- A Denial of Service to the previous (legitimate) phone owner while the new owner is using the phone to turn it into bots,
- Identity theft.

You see, if you sell your phone without removing all your personal data, you risk being linked to a criminal or terrorist act, and, although you will eventually be cleared, the process can be antagonizing and frustrating.

Second, physically clean the phone so it looks almost like new. There is a market for refurbished phones because buyers know they can save up to 33% on the retail price of a new phone. Another reason refurbished phones sell like hotcakes is because many consumers don't want to get stuck with a phone plan.

To get your phone refurbished, all you have to do is bring it to the shop where you bought it, to a repair shop, or to the manufacturer's store and request that it be restored to its original specs. That's all! This improves the value of the phone by at least 10%.

If you don't have a used phone lying around, you can buy them from relatives and friends for a low price, get them refurbished, then sell those.

Where to Sell Cell Phones

You can be the direct seller and go around offering the phones for sale or you can post your offer online. Multiple websites allow you to sell online as an individual and get paid online as well. A third option would be to bring the phone to a cell phone store or repair shop that buys secondhand gadgets. However, you probably will not get the best price by selling to a middleman because they need to make money as well by selling the phone in their store. The advantage of selling to a store is the quick cold cash given to you on the spot.

The websites where you can try selling phones are:

Amazon.com

Since Amazon is considered the leader in selling goods, used and new, your chances of unloading a cell phone are pretty high here. Set up an Amazon account, provide your US bank details and credit card information, and could be ready to sell in minutes. You should sign up as an individual seller and will be asked to provide your mobile phone number to get started. Plan out your strategy, take photos of your phone, or get a stock photo of the phone. You can even search for the same phone being sold on Amazon and copy the details found there for use as the description in your ad. When a buyer pays for the phone, Amazon will contact you to arrange delivery and payment.

Overstock or O.Co

Based in Salt Lake City, Utah, Overstock is now available to global customers. So, if you sign up to sell here, your item could be bought by someone halfway across the world from you.

The website will handle marketing as they email their thirty million subscribers regularly about the products on their site. On the downside, they do not have private auctions and cannot block bidders.

Registration is free, and the first photo you post is also free. Succeeding photos cost $0.10 each, and you are limited to uploading a total of seven photos. If you want to post even more photos, you must subscribe and pay a monthly fee of $6.95 for a maximum of twenty-five photos. The advantage of using this website compared to eBay is that any bidders must put down earnest money through their credit card if they want to bid. This ensures that the sale will push through. Bids that don't ultimately get the item will automatically be refunded. Seller gets paid through electronic transfer.

eBay

Everyone is familiar with eBay, which is an advantage from the get-go. You also can dictate how you want to be paid: via bank deposit, PayPal, wire transfer, etc. It's very easy to sell on eBay, and all you need do is register and set up your account.

Your old smartphone may be worth more than you think. People are willing to pay more than what a carrier is offering for a smartphone on eBay, as long as it is in good condition. Even if the phone is broken, some people are willing to purchase the phone for parts.

It is easy to see how much the device is selling for by simply searching eBay for other devices that are the same as yours. Make sure, when you search, that you only search for sold listings. This will let you see what amounts other sellers have received on their devices, what buyers were willing to pay, and enables you to set an appropriate price for your device so that it gets sold. Before you sell your device, make sure to wipe all your information from the phone and from the memory card.

Once you have decided to sell your device, you need to set up a free seller account. The account will allow you to list up to fifty items a month. Each of your listings can also feature up to twelve photos of the item you are selling. Be careful when listing an item; some of the available features cost extra.

eBay's web interface or app will automatically populate information about the device. It will also suggest prices to list the device based on other listings. When choosing what price to place on your item, if you are putting it up as an auction only, set the beginning bid at the lowest amount you are willing to sell the device for. You can choose to run your auction for one to thirty days; the choice is yours. Most sellers have their auctions run for at least five days.

The more items that you include in your listing, the better the listing will lure in potential buyers. For example, if you have extra phone cases, extra screen protectors, the original box, charging cord, earbuds, or other accessories, these things will make your listing more appealing than just offering the phone itself.

Make sure to take quality photos of your device and all the included items. It is important to take pictures on a clean surface and from every angle. People want to be able to see as much of the device as possible. Also make sure to take pictures of any scratches or flaws, and mention them in the listing. Make sure to take a picture of the screen with the phone on (if it is a working phone). You will also want to include in your listing if the phone's ESN is clean.

Other Sites

Other sites to consider are Best Buy, Newegg, Walmart, T-Mobile, AT&T, and your local flea markets or yard sales.

#5: Make Emergency Money with an Online and Off-Line Garage Sale

Cleaning out the clutter in your home or just getting rid of items that you no longer use is a great way to make extra money. According to statisticbrain, over 165,000 garage sales happen each week, and over 690,000 people purchase something at a garage sale each week, with 95,000 items being listed on Craigslist every week. Things like old but usable outdoor furniture, electronics, housewares, appliances, clothing, garden tools, and toys can be sold in as little as one day or two.

If you're considering hosting an online or off-line garage sale, here are some tips on how to make your efforts more successful and your garage sale more profitable.

Box up valuables. Keep a box and/or set aside an area in your home where you can stash the items you want to sell. As you go through your house, add items you want to sell to the designated box or area. Doing this over time, instead of last minute, will cut down on the stress and help you to not overlook things that can be sold.

Make items shine. Cleaning your items for sale will make a better impression. Getting rid of the dust and dirt will make the items look nicer, and customers will be willing to pay more.

Collaborate with others. Have a multifamily garage sale. Ask your friends and neighbors if they would like to join you in having a group garage sale. Customers are drawn to bigger garage sales because they feel they will have an easier time finding interesting items. Having a multiple-family garage sale is also a great way to add more foot traffic, which could mean more money for you.

Advertise your garage sale. You can take out a small ad in your local newspapers for your garage sale. Also you can utilize websites like Craigslist and Facebook to advertise the garage sale for free. You can also place signs around the neighborhood, advertising the date and time of your garage sale. Here are some great places where you can advertise your garage sale:

Gslar.com

This site is a garage sale, estate sale, and yard sale listing service. You can browse such sales by locating your city and viewing those that have been posted on the website. Use the map interface and trip planner to help you plan your weekend.

To sign up is free. If you wish to remove your ads, you can sign up to be a Pro member for $4.99. Users can also utilize the mobile app available for Android and iOS for when they are on the go.

It is free to list your garage sale, estate sale, or yard sale. This site has made it easy to list your sale and photos. You are allowed to add up to fifty photos of your sale items for free. For your ad posting, give the address and details of your sale. Your listing will also be posted on their company's partner site and be emailed to garage sale shoppers.

For more information, please visit http://www.Gslar.com

Yard Sale Search

This is one of the largest websites for garage sale and yard sale ads. Every month thousands of garage sales and yard sales are listed here. Simply find your city and state, and start searching. Users will also have access to yard sale tips and maps.

The website is free to use. You can list your garage sale or yard sale simply by supplying the address, details of the sale, and photos.

For more information, please visit: http://www.yardsalesearch.com/.

Recycler

This website was launched in 2010 and is a favorite between local buyers and sellers. Users who are looking for items can find services as well as new and used merchandise, such as cars, furniture, electronics, and so on. You'll also discover an easy-to-use search tool to filter and sort your search. Users can also set their location and save their favorite searches. Users can also request to receive email alerts when a new listing is placed for something they are interested in.

For those wanting to sell on this website, you should set up an account. You can use the ad creation tool, or the company is willing to design an ad for you. Users can place up to twenty-five ads per day.

For more information, please visit: www.recycler.com.

Determine how much you will sell your items for. Items such as paperback books usually bring about $0.50 each. A book that is autographed will bring in a higher amount. Pricing items above the minimum amount you are willing to take will give you room to negotiate with your customers.

Offer incredible deals. If you have items that you can sell together, list them as a super sale. Items such as a group of boys' toys or a group of weight equipment are great items to sell together as a set. You can also sell empty shopping bags for $5–$10, telling customers they can now fill their bags with as many items as will fit in the bag.

Offer snacks. Having simple refreshments will bring in customers and make them feel at ease, and they will be more likely to buy from your garage sale.

#6: Making Emergency Money with an Online Garage Sale

If you are not able to hold an actual garage sale, you can always sell your items online. A few sites allow you to post items for sale at no cost. Some of them charge a small listing fee and another fee when the item sells. Below are some well-known websites you can use for your online garage sale:

Craigslist

Craigslist was founded in 1995 by Craig Newmark and is headquartered in San Francisco, California. It is an American classified advertisement website with different sections for people to place ads for jobs, items for sale, personals, items wanted, even posting résumés and services.

As a user, select the city you would like to search. Each city or area has postings unique to that area. As a poster, you should decide which cities or areas where you would like to post your ad.

This website is absolutely free to use. However, you should sign up for a Craigslist account. There are no fees or charges for listing your items for sell. Make sure to take a lot of pictures of your items, and, if there is a flaw, make sure to have a picture showing it.

The site gets more than twenty billion page views per month. The site has a flagging system where users can flag posts that they believe to be in violation of Craigslist guidelines. Users do not have to be logged in to flag posts. If a post receives a certain number of flags, the system will automatically remove the post.

If you have more than one person interested in your item, it is best to follow the first come, first served rule. Keep a list of all the people who are interested in the item in case the first sale falls through. This way you can contact the other customers and let them know you still have the item if they are interested.

After you have agreed to sell the item, select a safe meeting place. Choose somewhere with a lot of traffic, especially if the item is a highly valued one. Note that some local police stations have areas for these transactions, so check with your local police, sheriff, and fire authorities.

Craigslist's URL is www.craigslist.org.

Amazon

Amazon is the largest and most valuable Internet-based retailer in the world and was founded in July 1994 by Jeff Bezos. Amazon is headquartered in Seattle and has even surpassed Wal-Mart in sales. Amazon has a customer base of around thirty million people worldwide. It began as an online bookstore and later went on to selling things like DVDs, audiobooks, video games, furniture, apparel, toys, jewelry, and food.

Some products are available for international shipping; however, there are separate retail websites available for those who live in the United Kingdom, Ireland, Canada, Germany, France, Italy, Brazil, Australia, Netherlands, Japan, China, Mexico, and India.

Amazon's URL is www.amazon.com.

Tips for Selling on Amazon

Amazon is the largest and most valuable Internet-based retailer in the world and was founded in July 1994 by Jeff Bezos. They are headquartered in Seattle and have even surpassed Wal-Mart's sales. Amazon has a customer base of around thirty million people worldwide. They began as an online bookstore and later went on to selling things like DVDs, audiobooks, video games, furniture, apparel, toys, jewelry, and food.

Some of their products are available for international shipping; however, separate retail websites are available for those who live in the United Kingdom, Ireland, Canada, Germany, France, Italy, Brazil, Australia, Netherlands, Japan, China, Mexico and India.

So here is a list of tips to get you started:

1) Register as a professional seller
   a) If you register as an individual seller, Amazon charges $0.99 per sale and a 15% commission for selling the item.
   b) If you register as a professional seller, you'll be charged $39.95 per month and a 15% commission for selling the product. However, you are not charged the $0.99 per sale.
   c) As a professional seller aka a pro seller, you can create listings for products not currently being sold on Amazon.
   d) There are several restricted categories. As a pro seller, you will be able to apply to sell in these categories.
   e) You must also be a pro seller if you would like to register your brand with Amazon.
2) Sell with FBA (Fulfillment By Amazon)
   a) This program will send all the merchandise you are selling to Amazon.
   b) Amazon will handle refunds, returns, communications, and customer service for you.
   c) Amazon will ship the item when it sells.
   d) Make sure to label your items and shipment correctly when sending them to FBA.
3) Follow the rules.
   a) Amazon has bunches of rules and regulations.
   b) They do not change their policies or rules often, so it is easy to follow and understand them.
4) Win the buy box to increase your sales.
   a) Be the lowest price, including shipping.
   b) Sell an item no one else has.
   c) Use Amazon's bundling policy to create unique items.
5) Make sure to answer customers quickly.
   a) It is suggested that you answer any customer questions within twenty-four hours.
   b) Not answering questions in twenty-four hours will cause your account to receive a demerit.
6) If you are a merchant, you should ship all orders within one business day and always enter tracking information.

7) Do not trust UPC codes when listing items.
   a) It is your responsibility to make sure that the item you are selling matches the item listed on Amazon.
   b) A lot of times manufacturers will update their products with new features, but they do not change the UPC codes.
8) Describe products accurately.
9) Ask for feedback.
   a) Customers will rarely leave feedback unless you ask them for it.
   b) There are third-party services you can use to email customers after they have made a purchase from you.
10) Use large images and follow Amazon's guidelines.
    a) Images must be at least 1006 pixels and taken on a plain white background.
11) Solicit product reviews.
    a) Ask your customers to leave a review about the product they purchased.

Amazon's URL is www.amazon.com .

eBay

eBay was founded in September 1995 by Pierre Omidyar and is headquartered in San Jose, California. It is an American multinational e-commerce company. They provide consumer-to-consumer and business-to-consumer sales services. It is now a multibillion-dollar business with operations in more than thirty countries.

Individuals and businesses can buy and sell products of a wide variety either through auctions or buy-it-now services. The website is free to use by those who are buying. The sellers, however, are charged fees for listing items and for any items that they sell.

eBay's URL is www.ebay.com.

To begin selling on eBay, you first need to register as a user and then click on the Start a Business Account link. Here you will enter your personal information and business name and type. You should name your business. Example, Mikeysonlinegaragesale.

You also need to sign up for a PayPal account. If you already have one, you can upgrade your personal account to a premier account. There is no fee for doing this. A few verifications steps are required to allow you to accept credit and debit card payments.

Your first fifty listings per month are free. After you have fifty listings, you will be charged $0.30 per listing. You will also be charged a 10% final value fee on the total amount the item sold for.

Here are some additional tips for selling on eBay:

Create proper and professional eBay listings. Make sure to take good pictures of your items. The more detail you can show buyers, the more likely they will view your listing.

Choose a good title. Make the title relevant for what you are selling. It should draw the readers' attention and make them want to click on the link to see your item.

Give a complete description. Make sure to completely describe your item. It is also important to state if there are any flaws in the items. For instance, list any cracks, stains, chips, etc. and include pictures of the flaws. You don't want the buyer to think they are getting something that is perfect when it's not. Be honest and don't mislead the buyer in any way.

Take incredible pictures. When taking photos of your items, it may be a good idea to include a name tag sharing the item name or number. Also print out a copy of your ad and put it with the actual item. Hopefully these double-checks will avoid sending the wrong item to the wrong customer.

Identify your shipping process. You should decide if you are going to include shipping costs in the price of the item or have the buyer pay for shipping separately. To ensure that you have the right amount of shipping on your package, pack up the item and weigh it on a postal scale. You can then purchase and print your postage label through eBay.

Promptly ship sold items. Once you have sold an item, prepare it for shipping. Take it to the post office or a UPS or FedEx office as soon as possible. Do not delay sending the item to the winner.

FAQs

What to Do If You Don't Have Any Items to Sell?

If you don't have any items to sell, you can visit different thrift stores and purchase items at a discount to resell for profit. (See retail arbitrage section for more information.)

How to Determine How Much to List an Item?

Did you know that there are annual updates on the selling prices for common garage sale items? For instance, books sell for around $1 which you can turn around and sell on eBay or to people you know for $5. Naturally some factors affect pricing, such as condition, author, and how many of its kind are on the market.

How Much Can You Earn from Garage Sales?

Countless stories abound of individuals who have been able to raise thousands of dollars on the junk of other people. However, it is important to have a strategy so your time is spent fruitfully.

First, know your market and what items they will buy in a snap. The last thing you want is to accumulate stuff in your home that you will not use and cannot resell. The list of garage sale items you seek should initially be typed out and brought with you everywhere you go. This leaves very little room for making mistakes, like buying the wrong item or dropping the ball on something that will sell well.

Second, learn to source garage sales not just in your immediate area but a little farther away, if possible. If you live in the city, you can turn a weekend into a treasure hunt outside your city. You can also scour online websites for secondhand goods to be bought online. Do not forget the classified ads in your local newspaper. This is still a fantastic source for information on garage sales! Also upper-scale communities tend to have better junk so this is a good target to source.

Third, plan your buying trip. You can opt to go to the farthest garage sale first or the most promising one first. Whichever you decide, make sure to get proper directions so you don't waste time (or money) finding the location. You should try to be onsite early for the first stop. This way you can look around, if allowed. Use your phone to take pictures of the most promising items and mentally figure out your budget as far as purchasing an item for resale and what you could eventually sell it for.

Fourth, wait for last-minute, frantic people holding garage sales who state, "I just want to get rid of everything!" People who hold garage sales tend to drop their expectations and prices right before they end their sale day. You might even get lucky to bag a wholesale deal if the owner just wants to get everything off his property!

Fifth, don't waste your time chatting with people or forcing a sale. If it isn't a good deal, and the quality is so-so, move on. You must take the stance of someone with a mission, although this does not mean being impolite, unprofessional, or pushy. Charm works better in this business, and you can get valuable insider information on other sales in the area by being nice.

Sixth, learn the art of haggling. Americans used to hate to haggle. However, recent studies reveal that over 70% of American buyers have haggled over a sale recently, more so because vendors are willing to negotiate. The best hagglers are those who have good personal relationship skills because they are diplomatic, tactful, but persistent. A great tip is to carry a lot of small bills because you can use it to negotiate for a lower price.

Seventh, buy quality products. With the intention of reselling what you buy, you need to determine the proper value and an item, and high quality is important. Thus, thorough inspection of all items is a must. The only exception to this is if you find something vintage with great potential. Then go for it!

#7: How to Make Emergency Money Engaging in eBay Retail Arbitrage

Arbitrage was a term used by finance professionals in the simultaneous trading of assets or commodities, like shares on the stock market. The seller acts as a middleman in generating interest and processing the transaction in order to profit from the different prices of the asset. For our purposes, however, *arbitrage* is the buying of items in one market (like Amazon) and then reselling the same item on eBay, and vice versa. Or to explain further, *arbitrage* is taking advantage of a slight price discrepancy that will allow the seller to pocket the difference by purchasing the item at a steep discount and then reselling for a profit. In essence, retail arbitrage is "flipping products online."

Quick Notes on Arbitrage

Before we get into the details on arbitrage, here are some quick facts you must know and understand about arbitrage to make a wise decision if this is what you want to do.

- The start-up capital requirement is about a few hundred dollars,
- Successful arbitrage requires close monitoring because prices can change at any time.
- There are fees to be paid on top of the price so, before you quote your price, take all these into consideration.
- There are risks in arbitrage, not just with the potential price adjustments but also in terms of your online reputation if you cannot deliver the goods or if the company that makes the product finds out and decides to make price changes to deter arbitrage transactions.
- Although there are stories of arbitrage millionaires, it is quite difficult to rely solely on this for a luxurious lifestyle.

- There are apps you can use to scan for low-priced products that can be resold for a profit.
- Arbitrage is not wholesale buy-and-sell because you are not transacting with bulk orders, so you don't have the extra advantage of a higher discount from the manufacturer.
- The profit margin for arbitrage can be as low as 5% but can go as high as 25%.

Amazon to eBay

Using these two popular websites can make arbitrage work simple and easy. You just have to search for products on Amazon and advertise them on eBay for a higher price. When an order comes in and is paid for, proceed to Amazon, buy it, and place the goods under the address of the buyer. Amazon will handle the delivery.

The advantage of this style is the low investment. You only need to set up your Amazon and eBay accounts, plus a payment option, like PayPal. The downside is that the amount you can make is small. However, you can systemize (automate) the process and make more that way by saving some of your time investment, depending on your skill, marketing, product line, computation, organization, and attention to detail.

Tools to Use for Arbitrage with Amazon to eBay

DS Domination

DS Domination is a membership training portal for those interested in home-based e-commerce. They have four basic training levels: Pro ($19.95/month), Elite ($99/month), Unleashed (a one-time $249.99 payment), and Monopoly (a one-time $499 payment). You can also be an affiliate and earn a 50% commission, but you must sign up as a Pro-level member first.

You are mainly paying for drop-shipping training. Many say that DS Domination is a scam because it offers very little information to nonmembers, and the website has been known to break a few Amazon rules. Also they mislead you about the "easy money" because drop-shipping entails a lot of work to be done to earn honestly using arbitrage.

ProfitScraper

Founded in 2014 by Anthony Hull, Profit Scraper offers its own software for arbitrage. This research app focuses more on individual sellers and gives you an inside track on profit levels and quantities sold. You have to pay $57 monthly, and you are confined to Amazon, not third-party sellers.

Profit Spy

One drop-shipping software that is getting rave reviews is Profit Spy. Although limited to the US market (which should not be an issue), Profit Spy delivers all that it promises. You will find thousands of items on Amazon that you can quickly flip for profit on eBay.

You can make anywhere from $5 to $20 on flipping products. Profit Spy has three monthly plans to choose from: Agent ($67/mo.), Detective ($97/mo.), and Secret Spy ($127/mo.). The differences in the plans can be found in the number of scrapped pages and add-on features.

You can decide to use none of these tools and work on your own, which means longer hours scouring Amazon but not having to pay monthly or annual fees.

#8: Getting Hired to Make Emergency Money

Secrets to Finding a Job Fast

Did you know that many people are looking for a first, second, or third job to make emergency money? Yes, it is true. There is nothing wrong with working one or more jobs to make ends meet. Over 70% of current workers are looking for another job even though a national survey pegs job satisfaction as of April 2016 as 88%. This only implies that workers know "something better is out there" and are willing to consider them. If you'd rather find a job than do some of the other methods mentioned previously, you should be able to find a job in fourteen days or less.

The rule of thumb in the job market is that, the more work experience you have, the longer it may take to find a job. This is because an experienced worker has higher expectations than a new graduate. Thus, if you're willing to take a job that doesn't require a lot of experience, then you can find a job quickly. However, you have to be focused and strategic in your job-planning efforts. Here are some tips:

Be Willing to Take Part-Time or Contract Work

According to Melanie Holmes of Manpower Group, "a contract position is probably the best way to get employed" because you gain access to inside information, not just about the hiring needs of the company but also the expectations and skills criteria. In addition, numerous companies are looking for freelance and temporary workers on a daily basis.

Use Your Skills to Your Advantage

Use your skills to wow employers and to seek positions you're qualified for. That is, if your skills are technical, then go for those technical jobs which utilize such skills. However, if you have no technical skills, then don't pursue positions where technical skills are required. Focus on what you are good at and market that. Be willing to adjust your expectations and to positively set forth your skills.

Use Your Network

Family, friends, and mates from college are people you can approach and inform about your job search. Most jobs are not posted on the Internet, so landing a job would happen more quickly with networking than with scouring the Internet. You should not pressure anyone into finding you a job, but you can let them know you are looking. Especially ask those who can give you references *and* are established in their field of expertise (which is your field as well).

In addition, if you do come across a job opportunity that isn't a good fit for you, pass the information to someone you know who could do the job well. This person will probably return the favor and do the same for you.

Tidy Up Your Social Media Accounts

Did you know that over 43% of employers check social media accounts of their applicants before making a hiring decision? Poor or questionable behavior on social media will immediately raise a red flag and put you out of the race regardless of your qualifications, grades, or any recommendations you may have used to endorse your application.

Behaviors that raise the red flag include:

- Inappropriate photos or comments,
- Poor choice of screen name,
- Willingness to share confidential information.

Dress to Impress

Finally stick to the age-old rules when going to an interview:

- Dress in proper attire,
- Make sure you are properly groomed,
- Arrive early,
- Bring a print copy of your résumé and reference letters and other supporting documents,

- Research the company and learn as much as possible about it,
- Never bad-mouth previous employers/schools/teachers—anyone!
- Be honest, sincere, and respectful.

#9: How to Make Extra Money by Finding a Job on Craigslist

Two sections on Craigslist are for someone trying to find a job: the Jobs section and the Gigs section. The Gigs section is primarily for someone looking for freelance work; however, employers will sometimes advertise job openings there too.

To get started, visit Craigslist.org and choose the city you wish to search for a job in. After you have selected a city, go to the Jobs or Gigs sections. The Jobs section will be divided into multiple categories, and, if you click the link to a category, it will show you all the jobs available in that category. You can also narrow the search within each category by selecting part-time or full-time. In the Gigs section, jobs are divided by types, such as babysitting.

The available jobs will be listed in the order of their posting date. So you will see the newest listings first, and each page will show about twenty-five listings at a time. Once you locate a job posting that you're are interested in, make sure the job is located in the area where you wish to commute. The ad will have two sections; the first describes the job, and the second section will detail the duties, contact information, qualifications needed, and sometimes the pay. Read through these carefully.

If you are interested in an available position, respond to the ad quickly—within forty-eight to seventy-two hours of its posting date. Some employers may receive hundreds of responses and may make their decision quickly. You should send them an email with your cover letter in the body of the email and your résumé as an attachment. This should be done through your personal email address, not any business email address you may use. If the employer has supplied an email address or a link to their website, make sure to use those instead of the general email supplied through Craigslist.

Unfortunately a lot of common scams are posted on Craigslist. Do not apply to any position that sounds too good to be true. If you still want to apply to the ad, do a quick Google search of the company name before moving forward. You can also send them a brief email, letting them know you are interested and would like more information. However, do not send your résumé or any personal information until you receive a legitimate response from a valid company.

Craigslist has become the place to go to find a job so plan to spend some time looking through pages of ads and choosing the ones you want to apply for. Just be careful and take your time. Read the ads thoroughly. And, remember, if it is too good to be true, it probably is.

#10: How to Make Emergency Money by Working for Temp Agencies

Working for a temp agency can be a great option for emergency money because these offices usually have an open door policy for applicants with little to no experience as versus the highly experienced individuals. It's quick income with many benefits, such as helping you update your work skills and expanding your network. If you are a new graduate, working for a temp agency will give you that most-elusive work experience that employers insist on before considering new applicants.

However, working for a temp agency also comes with its share of issues to be aware of in order to protect you from being victimized by unscrupulous persons. These issues are:

- Fake jobs, fake recruiters, both with the objective of stealing your personal information or building a database that they can sell to third parties,
- Supposedly guaranteed income,
- Top secret jobs with the government.

Best Tips on Finding a Good Temp Agency

Since over 80% of US companies prefer to use staffing agencies to fill any vacancies, why not ask what agencies they use so you can go straight to the source? This would require you to do some research online to find out the links between the companies you want to work for and their recruiters. This will also serve another purpose in that you are able to legitimize certain temp agencies from scammers.

Other tips on finding a good temp agency:

- Reliable temp agencies will always have information available about them. If you cannot find anything, then there is reason to doubt their legitimacy.
- A good temp agency is not just in the business of finding temporary workers for business clients but they also have to find a match for your credentials because you are also their client, a nonpaying client. This means you have rights and can negotiate terms of contract, work hours, and pay rate, especially if you have excellent work skills.

What You Should Expect When Working for a Temp Agency

Although the temporary staffing industry is a multibillion-dollar business, you can expect two challenges once you start applying with temp agencies.

First, it's not always easy to land the temporary job you want because the competition for jobs is fierce. To fight for your opportunity to work, beef up your skills, including interview skills. Dress the part, talk professionally, arrive early, and have the right attitude.

Second, you are likely to face discrimination as a temp worker. Unfortunately, because of automation, clients are able to be specific about what they want in their workers—including personal demographics, like race, religion, age, gender, or sexual preference.

This harsh reality does not have to affect you if you choose a temp agency with a solid reputation for fair play and employee protection.

Finally, do make it a point to find out the policies of each temp agency regarding applicants listing with various competing agencies, temp-napping, or agreeing to back-door hire. These policies have to do with ethical business practices. Not following these policies could result in your name being blacklisted in the temp industry.

#11: How to Make Emergency Money by Doing a Job

No One Else Wants to Do

Did you know that the riskier the job, the higher the pay rate? Or that odd jobs can bring in up to $80,000 a year for part-time work, like voice-overs by a noncelebrity? Odd jobs used to be income for new migrants, illegal aliens, or nonskilled individuals back in the day, but it is certainly not the case today! With the Internet and modern technology, it is actually possible to earn a decent living from odd jobs. Here's a clue: the cyber word for odd jobs is *freelance* work. Get it?

Some of the jobs that no one wants to do yet that pay good money include:

Trash Collector: *CNN Money* did a survey in 2015 and discovered—to their surprise—that a New York garbage driver makes an average of $112,000 a year, while a garbage helper can make $100,000 annually! Yes, these workers do have to deal with stinky garbage—and even human remains—and work graveyard shifts, but the six-figure income is nothing to sneeze at. The national average though is $40,000, but the requirements to qualify for this job do not even include a high school diploma. In addition, because it is a job not many want to do, the pay rate has increased steadily by about 18% since 2009. (Truck drivers have to have an unblemished professional driver's license.)

Handy Andy: You can earn quite a bit by completing cumbersome tasks for other people. For instance, you could offer to clean up your clients' garages or closets, decorate their homes for the holidays, offer to put up a ceiling fan or fix a door, even to clean up the dog poop in their yard. Basically you can offer to do those things that need to be done that most people put off. You can even post your services online and offer them citywide to increase your earnings.

Clean Gutters: Homeowners schedule an average of two to three gutter cleanings a year. It's expensive to have it done by a professional because of the risks involved. According to Fixr, the average rate for cleaning gutters is $90 per visit for two hundred feet of gutters for a one-story structure. This rate usually includes the cleaning supplies and materials. Professionals charge a higher rate for extremely dirty and clogged gutters. The cleaning of downspouts is not included in this rate, with each downspout averaging another $60 each.

Become a Friend for Hire: If you can hire an escort or a best man for a wedding, you can also hire a friend. By signing up with an app, RentAFriend.com, you can earn up to $50/hour to become someone's best friend to join them while attending events, reunions, and concerts. According to this website, if you accept jobs five days a week, you not only earn up to $2,000 plus tips but you also get free meals and a great way to network.

Dozens of such odd jobs are just waiting to be filled. All it takes is a little creativity, humility, patience, and the right work ethic.

#12: Selling Services via Freelance Websites Freelancing

A freelancer is self-employed and offers their services. Usually a freelancer will have multiple clients at one time. Some may think that freelancers work for free or next to free. However, that is not the case; a freelancer sets his or her own prices, services offered, and target market of clients. As a freelancer, you are free to set your own hours, working full- or part-time, and on the projects of your choice. Strong freelancers are business-minded, adaptable, creative, good negotiators, persistent, and self-disciplined.

There are several perks to being a freelancer. It is easy to get started as long as you know what skill you plan to offer to clients. You will want to create a LinkedIn profile and maybe your own website to showcase your services. While the marketplace for freelancers is competitive, the need for freelancers is large. You are also free to work where and when you want. Plus you can pick and choose which clients you want to work with. It is important to remember that it will take time to build a client base, and so work at the beginning can be irregular. The more you network, the better chance you have at finding clients. Also working on multiple projects and with multiple clients may take some juggling to make sure that you deliver the work to each of your clients promptly.

It is estimated that by 2020, 40% of the American workforce—or sixty million people—will be independent workers, such as freelancers, temporary employees, and contractors. There are more ways for people to work remotely now than ever before. People work from devices, apps, and other personal technology that lets the freelancer and the client communicate with one another from anywhere. Talent-matching platforms and coworking spaces are just two of the leading trends in the freelancer economy.

There are many companies that hire freelancers. Below you will find a list of a few of these:

- LiveOps
- BBC Worldwide
- Carolinas Healthcare System
- Creative Circle
- CyraCom
- About.com
- Havenly
- Isobar
- Intel
- Haynes & Company
- Judge Group
- Achieve Test Prep
- Hollister
- CleverTech
- Kaplan
- Overland Solutions
- FocusKPI Inc.

These are just a few of the companies who hire freelancers to perform tasks for them. Many companies out there are looking to hire freelancers. It will just take some time and dedication to weed through the companies and find which ones best fit the services you are offering.

Websites that Pay Fast

Amazon Mechanical Turk

Amazon Mechanical Turk was launched in November 2005. The system allows businesses and individuals to use their interface to have others perform tasks for them. The jobs listed on the sites are called Human Intelligence Tasks or HITs. Independent contractors are able to search through the HITs to find one that best suits them. Each of the HITs lists the price to be paid for completing the HIT. Surveys are the most common type of HIT. The amount of money you earn is dependent on how much time you put into working HITs.

Signing up to work for Amazon Mechanical Turk is free. It will take about forty-eight hours to be approved. They will ask for your social security number for tax purposes. You will start out on a probationary period. You should complete at least one HIT a day for ten days, but you cannot complete more than one hundred HITs per day. Also you cannot withdrawal your money until the ten days are over. You must also set up an Amazon Payments account. This is where your payment will go for the HITs you complete. You can either request to have your funds put on an Amazon gift card or to have it sent to your bank account.

Crowdsource

Crowdsource is a content mill where you have the choice of being a freelance writer or doing micro jobs. To get started, you should apply and choose which job you want to do. After you have made your decision, you must take an assessment text before you can earn money on the site.

Pay for micro jobs is usually not more than $0.10 each. The writing tasks are paid per word at a price of $0.02 to $0.035 per word. Payments are made daily through PayPal.

TranscribeMe

TranscribeMe is a company that provides transcription of audio and video files. This is a great place for freelance workers to sharpen their skills. As a transcriber you will listen to audio and video files and convert what is said to text. Most of the time the transcription is of public speeches, lectures, conference discussions, and conversations. You are free to choose as many tasks as you wish to do; there is no limit to the amount of work you can do.

You must go through a registration procedure, filling out your basic details and PayPal account information. You then need to take a transcription test, and, after your application is reviewed, you will be contacted through email.

You do not need to have experience to apply here. These are the basic requirements:

- Excellent typing skills,
- Speak and write English,
- Recognize American English accents.

Technical requirements:

- Fast computer or laptop,
- High-speed Internet connection,
- Chrome web browser,
- Headphones.

For general transcription tasks you can be paid up to $20 per audio hour. The amount of pay is also dependent on the length of the audio. You will be paid every Tuesday as long as at least $10 is due you.

Textbroker

Textbroker is a site for freelance writers. Thousands of writing orders are posted every day, and, as an author, you are free to choose which order you work on. It is free to sign up as an author as long as you live within the United States. When you apply, you will be required to send a copy of your photo ID to verify that you are indeed a United States citizen.

After you have completed your basic information, you will be asked to submit a writing sample. The sample should be between 120–250 words. You will be given a topic to write on. Make sure to take your time with your sample. The rating you receive will determine the types of assignments you can accept. You may only accept assignments at or below your rating. Here is a list of what each rating pays:

- Two stars: This is considered average. You will be paid $0.007 per word.

- Three stars: This content is *good* quality. Three-star authors receive $0.01 per word.
- Four stars: This is *excellent* content and pays $0.014 per word.
- Five stars: Authors at this level are considered professional writers. Unlike the other levels, you must pass an extremely difficult proofreading test in order to become a five-star author. At this level you are paid $0.05 per word.

Payments are made every Friday as long as you have at least $10 owed to you.

iWriter

iWriter is a platform where people can purchase articles that other people have written. It is easy to join this website. Simply sign up and fill out the form, then wait for your email confirmation. Once you have received your confirmation, you are ready to begin writing.

Now search the open index showing all the available orders. You can pick any article that is open and begin writing. You can only accept one article at a time. If a client likes your work, the client can send you special requests that will pay a little more than the usual articles on the index.

You will also be rated by the client on your work. Writers who have a rating of 4.1 or lower can only access the lowest-paying articles. Those who have a 4.1 or higher rating can choose articles from the lowest to the highest paying. Payments are made only through PayPal, and you choose when you would like to get paid. There are four options: the fifth of every month, the twenty-fifth of every month, every Tuesday, or every other Wednesday. You can change your payment options whenever you like. You must have at least $20 in your account to get a payout.

Transcribe Team

The Transcribe Team offers transcription service to individuals and businesses. They are located in Arlington, Virginia, and aim to give their clients fast, accurate transcriptions.

The only requirements that you need to work for them is a home computer and an Internet connection. You must fill out their online application and submit two transcription samples. You can choose your work schedule and work as little or as much as you want. The pay rate is between $0.40–$1.25 per audio minute, and you will be paid once a month through PayPal.

Clickworker

Clickworker is a company based out of Germany. Clickworker is similar to Amazon Turk. They pay people to perform short tasks using their computer. You log in and do as little or as much as you want. The amount of money paid per task will vary, depending on the project you are working on.

You will be paid either via PayPal or direct deposit. Payments to PayPal occur once a week between Wednesday and Friday, and direct deposit payments are made once a month.

NexusOP

NexusOp provides support services for clients who are based in the United States and overseas. They do not do cold calling. All the calls received are customers of existing clients. You will be answering their questions about products and services.

Requirements for this job include:

- Good communication and problem-solving skills,
- Quiet work environment,
- Must be at least eighteen years old,
- Computer or laptop,
- High-speed Internet,
- Headset.

Emergency Income Streams

The pay range is between $0.13–$0.44 per minute. You are only paid for the time you are on the phone with a customer. Payments are made every week through direct deposit.

#13: How to Make Emergency Money by Tutoring

Private tutoring is an excellent way to make not just emergency money but a full-time income as well. A private tutor earns an average wage of $16.80 an hour. On the high side, the earnings can amount to as much as $82,400 a year! Historically though, tutoring is known as a stop-gap career, meaning most tutors move on to other careers, like executive assistant, educator, even parenting.

Tutoring is not easy. You should be very well-versed in the subject you are to teach, and usually you will be called on to teach more than one subject—especially if you plan to offer your services to struggling high school students or those who want to qualify for GED credentials.

Qualifications of a Tutor

- Flexible work hours,
- Willingness to travel to teach or use technology (email, live chat, video chat),
- Excellent communications skills,
- Capable of breaking down complex problems for students to understand,
- Ability to adjust to each student's learning style,
- Create or source instructional materials to augment learning. This can be done by buying books on Amazon or eBay,
- Teach academics and good study habits,
- Simulate exam pressure with practice tests.

How to Get Started

1) Prepare your credentials. If you don't have anything but a college diploma, you can start by joining a tutoring service (care.com, preply, mathelf, TESTIVE, which is perfect if you want to teach students who fared poorly on their SATs), where you get invaluable experience and introduction to the work of a tutor.

2) Once you decide to strike out on your own, you must find students. Distributing flyers is very effective. You want to keep your marketing low-key because most parents do not want to broadcast that their children need tutoring. The best marketing you can hope for is word of mouth, so doing a great job will pay huge rewards in terms of new students.

You can also try posting your services online with reputable websites like CareerBuilder, Indeed.com, and Fiverr.

3) Consider offering special rates with group discounts or online tutoring which will not require you to travel. However, to do this, you have to set up an online payment system to ensure you get paid on time and without worries.

Since tutoring for the SATs and GED offers higher rates, you can benefit from a few tips, such as:

- You must have passed the SAT with flying colors or recently taken the SAT pretest and done well by getting higher than 1,500—which is the national average passing score.
- Purchase SAT/GED materials with sample questions.
- Know how to enhance the skills that you lack.
- Prepare short quizzes.

Finally, know as much as you can about these exams so you don't find yourself flat-footed when asked questions by parents or guardians.

#14: Emergency Money as a Babysitter

According to *Fortune*, American households are spending more on quality child care than on rent. In this situation, child care costs refer to day care or nursery school more than babysitting services. Babysitting costs take about 1% of the average family's budget. Parents are now considering a shift to babysitting services instead of day care because day care can currently cost more than a college tuition. In fact, based on research by the Economic Policy Institute, child care in a rural South Carolina town costs an average of $344 a month for a toddler and over $1,400 in Washington, DC!

Here's where you can come in and offer your babysitting services so parents can continue to bring in a double income without having to stretch their budget to accommodate day care. Babysitting has become an industry of its own, earning $1 billion from 2011 to the present. This industry is composed mainly of otherwise unemployed persons (so the babysitters have no other jobs to interfere with the childcare) or people who work solo.

The national average babysitting rate in 2014 was $13.44 an hour with a low of $10/hour, a 28% increase from 2009 rates. Last year, babysitters were more in control of their rates and observed an increase in tips and allowances. The average tip rate was around 26%, and 51% of couples preferred older sitters because of their experience and maturity as compared to babysitters still in school.

Basic Requirements to Be a Babysitter

A babysitter is a special job because it requires parents to trust their child with a nonrelative. The apprehension is understandable and justified. Thus, the first requirement, if you want to be a babysitter, is to have credentials.

Other requirements include:

- A passion for children plus patience,
- Training in CPR, safety, and basic child care,

- An even temperament,
- A flexible schedule,
- References.

How to Start Your Babysitting Service

Ideally you should have experience handling children and babies before you start marketing your services as a babysitter, so, if you can volunteer with your local church, day care, or even your relatives, do it. This will prepare you for dealing with other people's children and to minimize any fears you may have regarding your skills. Remember, you can learn babysitting skills, and the best teacher is experience. Some of the babysitting skills you can offer include:

- Helping with homework,
- Playing,
- Teaching a new language or skill,
- Being a vacation babysitting buddy, wherein you join the family on their holidays and help parents take care of the children while traveling.

The next step to take would be to research the rates in your area. It would be best to match or offer something a little lower to get your foot in the market. You could also charge a little more but offer extra services. Keep in mind that your rates should be higher for babies than for preteens, for obvious reasons.

Potential Companies Where You Can Work as a Part-Time Babysitter

Absolute Best Care

Member of the International Nanny Association, this company, based in New York, hires part-time and full-time workers. A part-time worker can earn as much as $700 a week. Acceptance is strict, and an application goes through a rigid background check and assessment. An online application is available.

Sensible Sitters

Present in seven states across the country, Sensible Sitters uses software for its referral services. The company has been around since 2005, and their goal is an educational-quality babysitting experience so children don't waste time while being watched. To join their team, you need to apply online and agree to a background check. Payment is done after the company gets paid by the client through electronic transfer.

Care.com

A familiar name in family and child care, Care.com offers a daily list of available jobs for empty nesters and those from the Catholic faith. Simply sign up with their website and gain access to dozens of babysitting job opportunities that can even include transportation and higher-than-usual hourly rates.

Other Babysitting Companies

Other companies looking for part-time babysitters are Guardian Angels Sitting Service, On Call Sitters, and First Choice Sitters. If you search the Internet, you will find many more close to your residence.

The bottom line is that babysitting is a low start-up business that relies heavily on your personality, trustworthiness, honesty, and discipline. It will also help you to get placed as a babysitter if you get health, hazard, and personal liability insurance and proper first aid training, available from your local Red Cross.

#15: How to Make Emergency Money by Going Door to Door Offering Handyman Services

Before getting into how you can make emergency money with handyman services, here's a caveat emptor: Just in 2016, the Better Business Bureau warned consumers to "Just say no" to door-to-door individuals who turn out to be con men. Gone are the days when a knock on the door is no reason to get your suspicions on red alert. Today, people peek through the windows, shout through the doors, or just ignore the knocks, especially if they are not expecting anyone because of the fear of becoming a victim.

That being said, there are still income opportunities when offering handyman services, provided you do it properly. For instance, start by visiting people who know you or your family, like your neighbors and relatives. As for homeowners who do not know you, pass out flyers first. Drop them in their mailboxes; distribute them personally while people are in the local grocery store or after church services. Become a familiar face to them and you can increase your chances of being accepted as their handyman.

Quick Tips to Closing a Handyman Job Contract

First, do the groundwork, which means having a rate sheet for the different services you can provide. Do not offer services you are not skilled at because it will ruin your reputation as a handyman. When preparing your rate sheet, you need to consider how to get back the money you invested for equipment but do not charge so high in a rush to recoup your capital. Also have the corresponding paperwork for job contracts which the property owner should sign to guarantee that you will be paid for services rendered. In some states, a contract is mandatory so might as well be prepared in advance.

Second, be ready to accept credit card and check payments. Many security experts have been telling consumers not to pay in cash because of possible scam issues. Thus, open an account where you can deposit the check payments or make arrangements for credit card processing through PayPal or other online billing services.

Third, don't be frustrated if you get turned down. Rejection will happen even for the most experienced door-to-door handyman. However, since most people prefer to be nonconfrontational, they will listen to your pitch before turning you down gently. Over time, you will learn the body language of a person interested in hiring you and learn to cut short your marketing spiel for those who aren't going to hire you.

Fourth, don't be a salesperson and avoid the hard-sell approach. Neither approach works well anymore and will make consumers think twice about trusting you. Just be honest, upfront, and sincere.

To be a successful handyman, become the person who can fix problems and solve emergencies, but you have to also be the one who does not overcharge or overstep the boundaries of a business relationship, unless invited.

Fifth, consider giving more than what is stipulated in the contract. Throw in some freebies, some minor jobs, like sweeping the sidewalk or mending a broken fence by renailing downed slats. Acts like these go a long way in establishing good rapport and a loyal customer base.

#16 Emergency Money as a Dog Walker or a Pet Sitter

Did you know that it is possible to earn a good income as a dog walker or pet sitter? According to a professional dog walker who has been in the business for the past ten years, it was awkward at the start with tons of skepticism, amusement, or plain disbelief, yet dog walking for $5 was the standard rate way back in the mid-1930s! In fact, in 1964, a highly respected businessman and heir to a well-to-do Manhattan family, Jim Buck, founded the Jim Buck's School for Dogs. Buck turned his back on his corporate career and established a successful dog walking business (and other dog services) that lasted for forty years.

With a pet residing in more than 50% of the eighty million US homes, a definite demand exists for dog walking and dog-sitting services. Business experts predict that the pet industry will be worth over $62 billion by end of 2016 or a 4% increase from the previous year. For pet services, the estimated revenue may be $5.73 billion, up from the $5.41 billion earned in 2015. Interestingly, use of pet services is sustained throughout adult life but peaks between the ages of fifty-five to sixty-four according to US demographic trends.

The trends are clear and fully support dog walking and pet sitting services. Some of these visible trends include humanization of pets, focus on the health and well-being of pets, and specialty pet services.

How Much Money Is in Pet Sitting and Dog Walking?

The average rate for pet setting is $15 per visit, while professional dog walking rates start at $18 for the first twenty minutes. Knowing what the professionals charge should make it easier for you to charge a little less as part of your marketing strategy. The amount you can earn will depend on how much time you are willing to allot to the part-time business. You can augment pet sitting and dog walking services with add-on services, like checking the house, feeding the pet, grooming, playing, charging special holiday and weekend rates, plus offering weekly or monthly rates.

You can also fix your rates so it conforms to specific types of pets since some animals are more high maintenance than others. For instance, according to *Canine Journal*, female dogs and puppies tend to be 15% more active than male dogs.

How to Get Started

It may seem like just a matter of making a few calls, but pet sitting and dog walking services mean you must be physically fit, a lover of animals, have a strong affinity with animals of all kinds, and have some marketing savvy. You can take a few shortcuts in your marketing by signing up with existing services.

Care.com

Care.com is in eighteen countries and has over twenty million members. They cater to almost all family needs, not just pet sitting and dog walking services. As a member, you get to see all available jobs with corresponding rates the clients are willing to pay. The average rate for dog walkers and pet sitters is $11.25 an hour.

It's free to join Care.com as an individual member, but you also have the option to sign up as a business member—which means you can post your services on the website and recruit people to work for you as dog sitters or walkers!

The company pays you through the WePay service, which is then deposited to your bank account without any fees. Care.com strongly advises against accepting cash directly from the client. They have good reasons for this, such as the paid memberships to their HomePay system that handles all your income taxes from the services you do with them to help you build your reputation, establish your home business as a sitter or walker, and even pay your taxes and that of your employees, should you decide to expand your part-time business and hire a team.

Pet Sitter

This is another website where you can post your services as a pet sitter or dog walker. Pet Sitter is part of the larger Care.com group.

Wag!

Wag! is currently in San Francisco, New York, and L.A., but they are aggressively looking for people from other states willing to start a Wag! in their area. Dog walkers get paid as much as $30 an hour. Their requirements are simple:

- Experienced in interacting with dogs,
- A passion for dogs,
- Trustworthy and willing to be accountable,
- Prompt, punctual, and can commit to a schedule,
- Good people communications skills,
- Able to establish rapport easily with dogs.

The procedure to get accepted as a dog walker is also quite simple:

1. Submit an online application,
2. Agree to a phone interview,
3. Pass a hands-on assessment test.

Other Websites

There are many other websites that can be used to market your services and many of them are free to register. You can also post your ads in vet clinics, groceries, churches, schools, or go door to door. You should invest in insurance and a license to operate unless you sign up with an existing business that will handle all that for you.

#17: Making Emergency Money via Entrepreneurship

Does the idea of working for someone else, even as a freelancer, seem unappealing? Perhaps you can become an entrepreneur. There are approximately twenty-eight million small businesses in the United States. Over twenty-two million of those businesses are self-employed with no additional employees. Small businesses have generated over 65% of the new jobs since 1995. Each month approximately 543,000 new businesses get started, and seven out of ten of those survive at least two years. Plus 52% of all small businesses are home-based, and 19.4 million businesses are sole proprietorships. As you can see, entrepreneurship is hot, and your entrepreneurial business efforts could lead you to a lot of money in both the short and long run.

Additionally the good news is that you don't even need a lot of money to get started. In fact, with perseverance, a will to succeed, special skills, and some creative marketing, certain entrepreneurial efforts could pay off big.

Here are some tips to help ensure that your entrepreneurial efforts are a success.

1) Make sure to have a written plan.
    a) Your plan should outline specific strategies, objectives, sales and marketing plans, financing, and the amount of cash you will need to get your business started.
    b) Writing down all these things is the first step in starting a business.
2) Don't marry your plan.
    a) Even though your plan may be very specific in how you want your business to run, realize that changes may be necessary.
    b) Be flexible when it comes to making changes to your plan.
3) Keep your ego in check.
    a) An advisor can help you inspect your business plan, and they can also give advice about ideas that you may have.
    b) Make sure to follow through on commitments, even if they are challenging and difficult.

4) Keep track of everything.
   a) If you are going to have others working with you, make sure you have a written orientation and training plan. This will ensure that your employees will know what is expected of them.
   b) Keep track of mileage. The 2016 business mileage rate is $0.54/mile. That's nothing to sneeze at if you travel ten thousand miles (or more) in one year.
5) Use the Internet.
   a) Use social media sites to network.

Mistakes will be made along the way. Learn from them. Your mistakes will be your best teacher in helping you move closer to success. Also you can learn a lot by simply listening to your customers.

Here are some great entrepreneurial ventures you can start today!

Make Extra Money Delivering Newspapers, Magazines, Etc.

Delivering newspapers, magazines, the *Yellow Pages* and other printed materials is a great way to earn extra money.

You can find listings for these types of side jobs in your local newspapers, or you can call newspaper or publishing offices near you to see if they are hiring independent contractors to deliver their materials.

For these types of side jobs, you will be required to have a reliable vehicle, current auto insurance, and a valid driver's license. Some places do have a minimum age requirement.

Product Development Corporation (PDC)

Product Development Corporation (PDC) is the largest phone book delivery company in the United States. They have been in business for more than seventy years. The company hires those who are at least eighteen years old with a current driver's license, a reliable vehicle, and valid auto insurance. You will also be required to attend a thirty-minute information session about what is involved and the delivery requirements. You must also obtain either a business card or an appropriate signature from all the businesses that you deliver to.

A GPS device is given to each distributor, which should be clicked when you have reached each delivery address. You will also be responsible for noting the Opt-Out address information for those customers or businesses who do not want the phone books delivered. You will be given a scheduled end date for when all your phone books should be delivered to the customers. This is typically three business days. If you are not able to complete your deliveries within that time frame, you will be required to call and keep them updated on your progress.

The amount of money you can earn is up to you. The more deliveries you make, the more money you make. Payments are made per address delivered to. Other things that determine the amount you are paid are book size and weight, and distance traveled. You can be paid four to five times a week.

Some of their distribution centers are only open certain times of the year. You can check to see if the distribution center near you is open by clicking here: http://www.deliveryellow.com/en/where-and-when

Newspaper Routes

Making newspaper deliveries can be a good way to earn extra income. The bigger your route, the more money you will earn. The routes will vary in customer size from thirty-five to seven hundred, where you could earn $150–$200 per week delivering newspapers. Some newspapers pay a set amount each week, while others pay an hourly rate or a set fee per paper. You may also earn tips from your customers from time to time. You will be working as an independent contractor and are responsible for paying taxes on the money you earn. You are also responsible for your own vehicle, including insurance, maintenance, repairs, and gas. However, remember that you can either get your business mileage reimbursed at the 2016 rate of $0.54/mile or you can use your car repair expenses as a business write-off at tax filing time, whichever is greater.

You can find ads for newspaper routes in your local newspaper, and also Indeed.com is another great resource for finding local newspaper routes.

#18: How to Make Emergency Money by Offering Services to Local Businesses

Local businesses are always looking for ways to save on operation costs which opens doors for you to make emergency money. You don't need surveys to tell you that small local businesses struggle to compete with national chains and their seemingly bottomless resources. In fact, with globalization and the ease of doing business today through the Internet, consumers tend to see local businesses as a "great idea but how long can they last?"

Here's where you come in. Do you have a skill that can be of use to a person running a business? Can you handle administrative work, accounting tasks, SEO jobs, or running a website? Are you good in sales and promotions or streamlining operations?

Here are some great ideas for making emergency money:

Offer Accounting and Tax Services: This service has become one of the most profitable for freelancers and part-time entrepreneurs—if you know the tax and IRS laws and have the proper credentials. Experts say it has a net profit margin of around 18%, which is more than what real estate brokers make. The cost to offering this service is minimal. You might even get away with using the small business's computer and working in its office, which would save you the costs of operating a computer, having Internet access, plus related office equipment and supplies.

Rent Your Car, Pickup, or Truck: If you have a vehicle you are not using, you can lease it to a local businessman or traveling business person. If you toss in the driver (that's you!), you get to charge more, plus tips. It is possible to link up with a car leasing company which offers on-demand services. Your costs to rent out your vehicle include gas, maintenance, insurance, detailing, and car washes. Of course, you need to factor in the depreciation costs as well, but it is possible to recoup all costs and to make money by:

- Selling mobile ads,
- Chauffeur services,
- Delivery services.

SEO and Specialized Design Services: With the competition heating up and the playing fields leveling because of the Internet, Search Engine Optimization (SEO) has become a highly sought-after service. Small businesses need this service to play with the big guys in their respective industries. The same applies for design services, which are flourishing because it adds value to a business at a manageable cost.

Instagram Consulting and Social Media Marketing: According to JWT Intelligence, Instagram use for businesses has been skyrocketing as evidenced by the jump in users to four hundred million in 2015. However, many of these business executives have no idea how to fully tap the potential of social media for their businesses, and they need help. Plus they are willing to pay good money, provided they get results. If you have experience marketing through social media, you have one of the top skills of our time.

Other Services: Other services you can offer local businesses are:

- Packaging redesign suggestions,
- Recycling suggestions,
- Software training,
- Becoming their mascot and endorser,
- Assisting with ground-level marketing.

#19: Emergency Money as an Online Bulletin Board Poster for People and/or Businesses Selling Stuff

Unbeknownst to many, software exists that can be used to set up an online bulletin board where you can make a little extra money selling other people's stuff. It's the electronic bulletin board system (BBS), and it is an online community where one can get the news, read ads, play games, and join in discussions or forums.

Most BBSs are operated by hobbyists, which means they do it because they want to give back to the community or because it fulfills an intangible need. You can use the BBS to offer classified ad services online, and you won't need much to get started. In fact, it can be done initially with a smartphone.

Your bulletin board advertising services should start with local businesses first because you can go door to door getting customers who may want to advertise but prefer not to pay the high newspaper classified ad rates. A good come-on to use in your marketing is to tell local business owners that, by advertising on your bulletin board, they increase their traffic as online bulletin boards are proven traffic builders.

A good starting point would be to get ten customers before you launch your bulletin board. To get the first ten clients quickly, charge low but charge monthly, like $5 a month for every ad. Be sure to stress that they can get tax credits for advertising, and, by being visible on your board, their businesses would go a long way in becoming a vital part of the community. You can also offer to have a real bulletin board placed in a strategic location known for a lot of foot traffic.

The Tricks to Successful Bulletin Board Systems

- Keep the online bulletin board clean and neat,

- Make all ads visible and easy to read,
- Keep a record of all your transactions and customers,
- Start a filing system so you can track customers' payments and dates of expiration for each ad,
- Update the board at least once a week,
- Add small snippets of interesting community data,
- Offer freebies in exchange for free publicity.

Here are some online bulletin board sites:

BBS Software

phpBB

This is free open-source software with a forum and bulletin board. The site has hundreds of designs to choose from so you can customize your board as you please. The beauty of this software is that it comes with a ton of information and help on how to get started—and they are constantly upgrading their system.

Simple Machines Forum

This is also free to use and can be set up in minutes. You are guaranteed complete control over your interactive forum and board. Some of its best features include:

- Multiple language support,
- Advanced user management,
- Quality SEO,
- Email, cookie, and session authentication,
- A ban-member option,
- Tracking and analytics,
- Guest mode.

bbPress **(Compatible with WordPress)**

If you are familiar with WordPress, then bbPress is a great choice. This free software is quite easy to learn and has fantastic integration. You can also divide your board into subsections and add plug-ins. It comes fully protected against spam.

Other Software

Other software to consider includes Zetaboards and PunBB, which are also free, or paid software like XenForo, Vanilla Forums, IP.Board, and vBulletin.

#20: Emergency Money as an Errand Runner

According to the Urban Dictionary, an errand is a task that has to be done often, something you don't want to do but have to. And herein lies an income opportunity if you enjoy running around: you can run errands for other people who prefer to spend their time doing other "more important" stuff.

Technically you can call yourself a personal assistant (PA), which has become an industry of its own. A personal assistant is different from a virtual assistant (VA), mainly because the PA runs errands and interacts with and on behalf of the employer/client, whereas a VA handles digital assignments that will not require any face-to-face interaction with the employer/client.

Characteristics of a PA

The traits a PA should have to encourage loyal customers include efficiency, self-motivation, common sense, organization, discretion, flexibility, good communication skills, adequate decision-making skills, discipline, and the ability to handle pressure.

In addition, one should expect all sorts of errands to run, from grocery shopping to paying the bills, picking up dry cleaning, or delivering packages (the holidays are coming up so this should be the busy time!). Naturally, as an errand runner, you have to set your own boundaries. For instance, the distance you are willing to travel, the jobs you are willing to do, and the rate you will accept as fair compensation for the work done. All these limits have to be settled before you start marketing your services as an errand runner.

Tips for Running Your Business

You can charge by the hour for your errand services and also charge for the mileage, adding that to your fee as well. Rates for running errands range from $20 to $40 an hour. You can also charge extra for holidays and after-hour errands or if the client wants you to do a rush service. Plus charge a fee if your client does not cancel your services within twenty-four hours. You can ask that your clients pay up front or pay on a weekly or monthly basis. Make sure to keep very good records for tax purposes to prevent any confusion come April.

Your primary goal is to get your name and services out there, so always be willing to do an exemplary job. Try to obtain as many positive referrals as you can. Always carry around a supply of your business cards and hand them out to potential clients. Don't be afraid to place a simple flyer in grocery stores or coffeehouses. You can also run an ad in the local newspaper or other daily publications. You should start out running your ad every week so that people will get used to seeing it and will know what services you offer.

After you have gained a few returning clients, you can then start offering them packages that come with a fixed rate for running their errands. You can choose what the packages cover—a month, ten hours, five hours. It is up to you. This will also allow for you to get paid up front and to know how much work you can expect in the future.

If you prefer to simply sign up with a company and sort through their listings of available clients and projects, here are a few companies that you can use:

Task Rabbit

Task Rabbit is very popular for several reasons. Its stringent requirements to become a Tasker include a background check, orientation, and interview. Every task is insured up to $1 million, but a Tasker must work hard to get rated to qualify for the higher-paying jobs. Tasks can be hourly or by appointment. The arrangements would depend on your negotiations with the customer.

Payment is done in cash immediately after the task has been completed successfully, although you can request for payment to be deposited to your debit or credit card. To sign up, register online and attend the orientation. To get tasks after you have been accepted as a Tasker, you need to download the app. Tasks are posted hourly and are based on your location.

Simply Hired

This is a search engine for different kinds of jobs, including running errands. The company gets around thirty million visitors a month and has been at the receiving end of gossip that it will be acquired by a larger company. However, so far nothing has come of the buzz, and there are jobs to be found here.

All you have to do is go to the website and search for errand running. The company has a salary calculator to help you determine if the offer being made is fair or not. The website is free to use.

Agent Anything

This website caters only to university students looking to make extra cash. To sign up, you need to register using your personal school email address and have access to a computer. Once you are accepted into the system, you can see what missions are available for you—those within minutes of your location. Every mission has its budget so you know immediately how much you will get paid if you are assigned the mission. Payment is through PayPal after the task has been successfully completed.

Zoom Errands

Zoom Errands is an errand provider, established in 2010 in Los Angeles. This is a fully managed company, which means, even as a part-timer, you get the full backing of the company.

To become a part of Zoom Errands, you need to register online and agree to an interview to get clearance. One of their prerequisites to getting clearance is previous work experience and appropriate skills. Once you have this clearance, you can accept jobs posted on the website. The company requires punctuality and responsible execution of every task. They also demand that you be professional but friendly with clients and able to communicate effectively with them.

Other Companies

Other companies you can consider are Door Dash (food delivery), and Instacart (grocery shopping), and SnagAJob.com (which requires a valid email address and updated SnagAJob account. You have to be a US resident and willing to start immediately. Their services are free to use).

#21: Emergency Money as a Housekeeper

In the United States, a housekeeper makes an average of $9.82 an hour and not always with benefits. The lowest you could get paid as a part-time housekeeper is $7.80 and the highest would be around $15.32—according to a national poll. The rate would depend on your location as major cities lean toward higher rates. The good news is payment is in cash immediately after the day's work is done or can be according to other arrangements made between you and the home owner, which means weekly or monthly.

Job satisfaction is also high, especially among women housekeepers, as they have almost complete control over their time and schedule.

The Duties of a Housekeeper

It is important to know what a housekeeper does because some employers like to take advantage of the situation and request housekeepers to do more than what their job scope entails. This isn't to say that you should not help in case of an emergency, but some tasks are not meant to be done all the time. Here are the typical housekeeper duties:

- Clean,
- Replenish supplies,
- Change beddings, towels, and do laundry,
- Minor repairs, like replacing busted or burned-out light bulbs,
- Reporting damage or anything that needs further attention.

Tasks You Can Charge Extra For:
- Tidying up closets and cabinets,
- Cleaning up after pets,
- Running personal errands,
- Cleaning the inside of large kitchen appliances, like ovens and refrigerators,
- Cooking.

Requirements to Qualify as a Housekeeper

It does not require much to qualify to be a housekeeper. You will only need to be:

- A US citizen or have a work permit,
- Eighteen years old or older,
- A high school graduate or its equivalent,
- Physically fit,
- Trustworthy and honest,
- Disciplined and organized,
- Punctual.

Where to Find Part-Time Housekeeping Jobs

Here are some websites you can use to find the housekeeping jobs closest to you.

Care.com

The jobs posted on this site offer rates from $10 to $30 an hour, which are higher than the national average. The higher rates in that range include additional tasks, like help moving in or help caring for kids or driving them around, so be sure to read the entire job description before applying.

To apply, you must first sign up and complete your online Care profile. Payment is made through direct deposit.

Merry Maids

This is a business with 1,351 franchises across the USA and Canada. Working with Merry Maids is a bit complicated because you may end up with a franchise overseeing you, and the franchises are allowed to set their own requirements for hiring full- and part-time workers.

The first step to apply as a housekeeper is to visit the website and sign up online. You will then be directed to the office nearest you.

ServiceMaster

ServiceMaster is the umbrella company to ServiceMaster Clean and Merry Maids, aside from other brands. The difference between ServiceMaster Clean and their Merry Maids' brand lies in the job scope. With ServiceMaster Clean, the work is janitorial: cleaning of floors, upholstery, and tile. It's very specific, and so, if you want to make sure you don't have to run personal errands, do any cooking or cleaning of personal belongings, instead of Merry Maids, go with ServiceMaster Clean.

The rate for cleaners is $9.37 an hour although, if you are labeled a "janitor," you get paid lower at $9.31 an hour.

The Cleaning Authority

The Cleaning Authority is another business with several franchise owners. All employees have to wear a uniform and work in teams. They have to follow the "no eating, no drinking, no smoking" policy of the company while working. All employees are fully insured and paid according to the franchise pay schedule.

The difference in working for The Cleaning Authority is that you will never have to do carpet cleaning, laundry, dishes, or wash windows. The work is strictly limited to cleaning the interior. If accepted, you have to undergo professional cleaning training and on-the-job training (OJT) before you are assigned jobs. They have promotions and rate increases that depend primarily on experience and feedback. However, each franchise may have different employment and promotion criteria from that of the head office. The basic requirements are good work ethics, the ability to work as a team, and a commitment to customer service.

#22: Emergency Money as a Gardener/Landscaper

Do you have a green thumb? This is a gift, and you can earn emergency money doing something you love: gardening and landscaping. On the Uptown website, which is a place where jobs are posted for freelancers, clients are willing to pay anywhere from $200 to $1,000—just for the landscape design! Professional gardeners charge around $55 an hour for their services, so, if you charge 10% to 20% lower, you have a great chance of booking customers. There is money to be made with part-time gardening and landscaping.

In December 2015, the *Chicago Tribune* came out with an article about gardening tips for 2016. According to Beth Botts, the most difficult challenge in starting a gardening business is having the confidence to do it. She says that first-time gardeners "learn that they can't control everything, but they can handle anything" because plants will grow back, so they get a chance to fix mistakes.

How to Get Started

Even if you have a green thumb, it's best to consider improving your credentials before you start marketing your services. You can do this by:

- Becoming a volunteer gardener,
- Joining a gardening club,
- Visiting gardening trade shows,
- Taking a class,
- Studying light, soil, and seeds,
- Reading,
- Starting your own garden.

What You Need to Do

A gardener has to be adept at pruning, mowing, weeding, sowing, raising plants, and tidying up gardens and pathways. You also need some skill in handling gardening tools, like the mower, shears, rotavators, saws, spades, and other mechanical tools. It will also come in handy if you know simple carpentry work so you can offer to build a shed or gazebo for a fee.

Most professional gardeners work up to forty hours a week, including weekends and holidays. As a part-time gardener, you have the freedom to choose your working days and to set your own hours. However, you should be flexible with your schedule as gardening is highly dependent on weather conditions.

Before starting, get a physical checkup by your doctor to make sure you can handle the physical demands of the job.

Organizations You Can Join

Several groups can help you get started as a part-time gardener.

The National Gardening Association

Established in 1973, the NGA has a mission to cultivate new gardeners, and help get them established and become better in their chosen hobby/job. Their members have access to a vast array of resources, a massive library, and highly technical advice from other members on gardening.

You can become a member by applying online. Best of all, they don't charge for membership!

American Horticultural Society

The AHS is a nonprofit group committed to the art of gardening. Members get access to their vast resources, facilities, and a subscription to their magazine. They operate River Farm, a twenty-five-acre property in Washington, DC, and home to the group's headquarters. Membership fees start at $35 and can run all the way up to $500. However, if you don't want to be a member, you can still visit River Farm, which is open to everyone, free of charge.

Gardeners Connect

GC is based in Kansas and currently has over six hundred members. Members enjoy benefits such as a bimonthly newsletter, garden parties and other events, discounts on gardening classes, field trips, and special discounts from their partner retailers or fellow members. Membership fees start at $30 a year and can go as high as $500 for a lifetime membership.

Lastly you can join an affiliate, of which there are dozens, offering special discounts and promos for its members. With affiliates, you can earn extra income by marketing their products while you do your gardening, so you get an opportunity to earn a double income with every job you book.

#23: How to Make Emergency Money as a Pressure Washer

Making emergency money offering pressure-washing services in your neighborhood is an excellent idea! Based on a 2015 survey, Americans spent around $299 to $561 just on having their roofs cleaned. The lowest amount paid for roof cleaning was $153, and the highest amount paid for the same service was $815. That's a lot of income opportunities just waiting to be made if you can get hold of a pressure washer, and learn how to use it effectively and properly.

The price of pressure washers has gone down to around $150, but only 15% of US households have their own unit, which means a gap still awaits to be serviced. However, an interesting trend has been observed. Even though people own their own pressure washer, they don't always take it out and use it for several reasons:

1. They don't have the time.
2. It's broken and expensive to repair.
3. Fear of using it because of news that it is potentially dangerous, especially if you use the red-colored nozzle—being too powerful, as made the subject of a consumer alert last July by *Consumer Report*.
4. They used it and damaged property because they could not control the power of the water.

How to Start a Pressure-Washing Sideline Business

Whether you want to do this one time or you're thinking of starting a sideline business, there are many ways for you to earn money with a pressure washer. However, before you go house to house, offering your services, a few basic requirements must be fulfilled.

First, get access to a pressure washer. You have two options: buy or rent. Home Depot and other similar stores offer rental services. To give you an idea of the cost: for an electric pressure washer, you will have to put down a $75 refundable deposit and then choose a time-based plan. The minimum is a four-hour rental for $26. If you want to get it for the day, you need to pay $37, while a week's rent would cost you $148.

You can buy your own for about $100 and higher, depending on the model. However, the low-end products tend to be more expensive to repair and generally have a reputation for being throwaways. You also have the choice of buying new or used, so you can buy something worth $500 for just $350 if you are resourceful.

Second, take time to learn how to use a pressure washer. There are different tips for the washer that are distinguished by their color. The universal codes are:

- Red: most powerful, used for metallic and concrete areas but from a specified distance.
- Yellow: Gives a fifteen-degree angled spray pattern and used for heavy duty areas like garages and roofs. This nozzle is not advisable if you plan to use a cleaning solution with chemicals because it is hard to ensure that the residue does not stick or enter crevices and cause damage.
- Green: This tip sprays at a twenty-five-degree angle and is great for decks, patios, and walkways. You can also use this for outdoor furniture.
- White: The spray of this tip is angled at forty degrees and is perfect for delicate surfaces.
- Black: This tip has a sixty-five-degree angled spray pattern and is recommended only for wetting surfaces before you apply the cleaning solution.

Third, some states require registration, an environmental permit, bond, insurance, and license before you can offer pressure-washing services so be sure to check with local authorities about the requirements for your area.

Fourth, create a marketing plan. Door-to-door canvassing works because it's personal and a lot of people like this old-fashioned way, plus you have the added advantage of impulsive consent. Consider buying print and online ads, plus passing out flyers.

Your start-up costs do not only include the cost of the pressure washer and cleaning supplies. You should also factor in the permits and licenses, and the transportation cost to get the washer to the job sites.

Fifth, once you get clients, work to turn them into regulars by providing excellent service, no back-jobs, and zero damage to property. Pretty soon the word will spread about your side business to the point that you may be tempted to leave your day job!

#24: How to Make Emergency Money Selling Scrap Metal

This one may seem ancient, but recycling can still bring in wads of cash. Plus, when metal is recycled, we reduce the amount of ore drilling throughout the world. Some of these metals include iron, aluminum, steel, copper and even wires. By recycling metal, you'll not only improve the environment but you will be making money at the same time.

Your local scrapyards offer payment for any metal that you bring into their facility. Before you head off there, the metals must be separated into ferrous and nonferrous metals. The easy way to remember which is which is to take a magnet with you. If it sticks to the metal, it is ferrous. This could be things like steel and iron. If the magnet does not stick to the metal, it is nonferrous. Nonferrous metals are things like aluminum, brass, copper and stainless steel.

These types of metals are worth more money at the scrapyard.

Copper is the most valuable metal to recycle, which is approximately $2.85 per pound. Aluminum is approximately $0.50 per pound. Steel and other nonferrous metals pay approximately $10 per pound. Other things to consider taking to the scrapyard are washing machines, dryers, refrigerators, stoves, gas grills and cast iron bathtubs. The amount of these items will vary from scrapyard to scrapyard.

It is possible to make $100–$200 dollars a day simply scraping metal. Things you will need in order to start are:

- A trailer with a ramp. Unless you are okay with scraping the bed of your truck. The metal or cast iron will scratch the paint, and it can be difficult to get some of the larger items into the back of a truck.
- You can visit Craigslist and search the free section for ads where people are giving away scrap metal to those who are willing to pick it up.

- Establish a relationship with the maintenance person in an apartment building. Let them know that you are willing to take away any scrap metal.

There is no minimum amount of scrap metal required before you head to the scrapyard. They will buy any amount you bring. Remember, if you are taking lawnmowers or other things that may have gas or oil in them, you will need to drain those liquids before you take those items to the scrapyard.

#25: How to Make More Emergency Money at the Recycling Center

Do you want a cleaner environment? Do you, your neighbors, family, or friends have items that can be recycled? If so, you can make cold hard cash by recycling, baby. Recycling materials not only keeps waste out of landfills and protects the environment but it can also make you some nice spending cash. Here are a few things that you can recycle:

Paper

Recycling scrap paper and cardboard from offices, homes, and other sources can make you some money. Because of the relative abundance and weight, mixed paper brought into the recycling center is worth about $45 per ton. However, clean white paper is worth approximately $200 per ton at some centers. You could also make deals with businesses to collect and dispose of their paper waste, and you can always ask family, friends, and neighbors to sort their paper for you to collect.

If you subscribe to any daily newspaper, you can get a portion of your money back by selling your old editions. Newspapers of today use plant-based inks, so no reason to worry about cross-contamination. Magazines, old books, cereal boxes, gift wrap, and egg cartons also fall under this category when recycling.

Aluminum Cans

This is one of the most widely recycled items in the United States. A single aluminum can is worth between $0.01 and $0.02. If you can hold off taking the cans in or collect one ton of cans, you could make approximately $2,300. You can find aluminum cans in recreation facilities, local parks—even start an aluminum can drive in your community.

You can also take in other types of scrap metal, such as copper, steel, and iron. Steel can be found in things like old automotive parts and appliance casings. Scrap steel is worth about $500 per ton. Copper is worth more than steel and can be found in things such as wires, electrical components, air-conditioner coils, connectors, and plumbing pipes. The amount paid for copper is approximately $3 per pound.

Plastic Bottles

Plastic bottles used for beer, soda, or water can be recycled at many recycling centers for cash. The triangle marked on the bottom of the bottle identifies what type of plastic it contains. Type 1 bottles are worth approximately $500 per ton, and Type 2 bottles are worth approximately $800 per ton. Some states have bottle deposit programs. Usually each bottle earns you $0.05 to $0.10 per bottle, depending on the area.

Other types of plastics that fit into this category are containers, plastic utensils, bags, and cups, including Styrofoam.

You can make some extra money by simply recycling everyday items. It takes some time, effort, and patience, but it pays off in the end.

Scrap Metal

As discussed in the previous chapter, scrap metal can be recycled and typically includes used wires, brass, iron, steel, and copper. Ferrous metals (those that attach to a magnet) do not sell for as much as nonferrous metals, but you can still get some cash for them.

As of November 2016, the price for ferrous scrap metals per one hundred pounds is $1.25, while, for nonferrous scrap metals, you can earn up to $2. Did you know that Christmas lights are considered copper scrap and can get you around $0.21?

Electronics

Electronic scraps are also worth some money. For instance, an old mouse or keyboard gets you around $0.04 while a CPU processor is worth $20. Old cellular phones can also be recycled, and they are being bought for around $3.40. However, if your cell phone is still in good working condition with minimal damage—and the battery still works—you can get much, much more. In addition, the charger can be sold separately or kept for use with other phones or as an emergency backup.

Your old SIM cards are also worth some money because they actually contain precious metal. Cash for Electronic Scrap USA is one website you can turn to for all your old electronics. This company even offers to cover the shipping and insurance costs. After they receive the items, wait ten days and then expect your check in the mail. Their reputation is impeccable.

Earlier this year (2016), Apple released a news report that they had recovered over 2,200 pounds of gold from old recycled iPhones, iMacs, and iPads. This gold brought in $40 million in fresh assets to the company. Aside from gold, these products also contain steel, plastic, silver, aluminum, glass, and copper. In total, the company collected ninety million pounds through its recycling program. This should give you an idea of what you can get from old phones and computers.

Wine Corks

Although recycling centers may buy your old wine corks for a small amount, you may also sell these corks at online sites, like eBay. The going rate for old corks is $0.10 apiece and bought mainly by crafters. Consider a craft store as your modern-day recycling center because they might buy your old craft supplies, like buttons, lace, ribbons, and other similar items.

Other items accepted at recycling centers are wood pallets, glass, ink cartridges, carton, and batteries.

Things to Remember When Obtaining Recyclable Materials

Certain items cannot be recycled. These include: Pyrex glass, foil-lined bags, lightbulbs, diapers, batteries, oil, cleaners, paint, and any cardboard that has grease or food on it.

You can prepare aluminum cans for recycling by rinsing them first so they don't attract bugs. Then either crush the cans to save space or leave them uncrushed.

Prepare cardboard boxes by removing any other materials therein, such as plastic bags, peanuts, etc. Break down the boxes to save on storage space, and try to keep them dry and free from oil and other contaminants.

Rinse glass containers with water and avoid breaking the containers so the glass doesn't mix with other types of glass. You do not need to remove the labels from glass jars.

How to Find Reputable Recycling Centers

To find recycling centers near you, go to the website called Earth911.com and type in what type of material you want to recycle plus your zip code, and the site will give you a list to choose from. Remember, not all locations offer cash for recycling.

Here are a few recycling centers that pay for recycled materials:

Downtown Metals & Recycling Center is located at 526 S. Alameda Street, Los Angeles, CA 90013. Phone: 213-625-8165. They pay $1.80 per pound for aluminum cans, $0.104 per pound for glass bottles, $1.19 per pound for plastic bottles, and $0.56 per pound for #2 HDPE plastic.

Baldwin Hills Recycling is located at 5080 Rodeo Road, Los Angeles, CA 90016. Phone: 323-784-9584. They pay $1.57 per pound for aluminum cans, $0.104 per pound for glass bottles, $1.19 per pound for #1 PETE plastic bottles, and $0.56 per pound for #2 HDPE plastic.

#26: A Crazy Idea:

Emergency Money for Plasma Donations

Plasma is the clear precious blood component that can be drawn safely from an individual to help another human being with medical issues. In fact, plasma can help a person suffering from brain disorders, blood clots, infections, liver disease complications, blood disorders, post-surgery complications, and kidney disease, among others.

It is common practice among struggling college students and those without jobs to sell their plasma. They can earn up to $70 weekly with minimal side effects unless you donate too frequently. Donating your plasma is done via insertion of a needle and is very similar to donating blood, albeit with a larger needle. The instrument separates white and red blood cells and the platelets immediately from the plasma, then the blood—without the plasma—is reinjected into the body. Unfortunately for those who need plasma, plasma cannot be produced in a lab nor can we use plasma from animals.

Is It Safe?

Yes, donating plasma is safe—both for the person donating and the recipient. However, donors must first undergo screening to test the viability of their donation and whether they can physically handle the changes in iron levels and blood pressure. Persons with preexisting medical conditions are generally discouraged or ineligible to donate plasma.

Experts say that around 40% of those who donate experience minimal side effects, like dizziness or moments of weakness. More serious temporary side effects are nosebleeds, colds, fatigue, fainting, and lowered immunity, although donors are required to eat and drink immediately after a donation to replenish the nutrients they lost. Frequent donors also get scarring from regular insertions.

In the United States, an individual can donate plasma an unlimited number of times, although generally the maximum should be once or twice a week. Red Cross will only allow once-a-month donations. A frequent donor should also take a break after selling plasma for three months to give a chance for his/her body to fully recover. A side note to remember is that plasma donors are not eligible for blood donations.

How to Get Started

The basic requirements, aside from the physical exam, are:

- Must be at least eighteen years old but not older than sixty-nine;
- Must weigh at least 110 pounds but not more than 400 pounds;
- In some states, must produce written consent if below a certain age (under twenty years old).

The night before you go in for a plasma donation, you must avoid caffeine, cigarettes, and alcohol. You must also be sure to eat a proper meal and get enough sleep. Three hours before the donation, drink at least three eight-ounce glasses of liquid, preferably water or juice.

After the donation, replenish by drinking more water or juice regularly for the next four hours and eating a light meal. Remove the bandage only after several hours, and, if you feel any serious side effects, return to the center and consult with the doctor.

Plasma Rates

Not every donor gets paid $70. Some companies only pay $20 and an extra $5 if your blood has a specific antibody they need. You may find coupons online that can be used to increase the payout amount, but, if you decide on Red Cross, you will not get paid at all since this is a charitable organization and a not-for-profit business.

Some businesses will pay you more if you weigh more because you have more plasma to be harvested.

Payment is usually paid via your debit cards and done on the same day of the donation.

Finding a Donation Center

For most plasma donation centers, you will be required to present the following:

- Social Security number,
- Proof of residency,
- Valid ID.

Pregnant women and anyone taking drugs are automatically disqualified from being plasma donors.

CSL Plasma

You need to go to a CSL Plasma center and present the requirements listed above. If accepted, you will be interviewed and undergo a physical examination. If the doctor says you are eligible for plasma donation, you will be directed to the room with the plasma machine. A plasma donation takes about ninety minutes to complete.

CSL Plasma has a rewards program called iGive Rewards, a loyalty program where you earn credits for every completed plasma donation. The credits can be redeemed at any time for cash, Deals of the Day, or other promotional items. The more plasma you donate, the more credits you will receive. As you earn more credits, you will gain a higher status: bronze, silver, gold, and platinum. To reach one of the higher statuses, you must receive all your credits between January 1 through December 31 of the same year. Membership levels are reset at the beginning of each new year. Your credits will be automatically uploaded into your account about seven days into the following month.

Credits on your account will expire if there is a thirty-day lapse in plasma donations. You must also login to your account at least one time every six months to avoid having your credits expire. They will continue to expire until you either donate plasma again, or, if credits are expiring because you have not logged into your account, they will continue to expire until the next time you login.

Once you have signed up for iGive Rewards, you can login to your account by using the last four digits of your Donor number (obtained from your plasma donation location), plus your last name and date of birth. Once you are logged into your account, you can choose to opt-in to receive emails and/or text messages about current and upcoming promotions and special offers in your region. You can also receive messages to let you know if your plasma location is closed due to bad weather. Your account information includes your donation history, membership level, account activity, and surveys. For more information on the iGive Rewards program,

https://www.cslplasma.com/current-donor-rewards/iGive-rewards

Octapharma Plasma

Octapharma has the same procedure as CSL Pharma and will issue you an Octapharma Visa debit card where your donor payment will be deposited. They pay $50 but require you to come in twice because the first donation merely tests your plasma and can only be used by them after the second donation.

Octapharma also has its rewards program called OPI Rewards. Loyalty points can be converted into e-gift cards, sweepstake tickets, or Express Passes. You can also earn points under their referral program. You get one point for every successful donation and an additional one point for every referral.

GRIFOLS

GRIFOLS also pays using a debit card. Unlike the first two plasma centers noted above, GRIFOLS uses a computer-assisted interview app to screen donors. This is found in their Donor Doc touchscreen kiosks that will ask you to answer several questions. According to GRIFOLS, a person can earn an average of $200 a month with regular donations, and payment is made on the same day as the donation.

#27: A Crazy Idea:

How to Make Emergency Money Selling Your Hair

If you have long hair and you are looking for extra cash, selling your hair could be the answer. The best hair extensions and wigs are made from human hair. Healthy hair is in high demand and pretty easy to sell online. Your hair could be worth hundreds or even thousands of dollars to the right buyer. Those that are looking to buy hair want thick, healthy, virgin hair that is at least ten inches long. They will not accept hair that has been permed, bleached, dyed or subjected to heat. They will also reject your hair if you are a smoker.

Here is how to start selling your hair online to make emergency money:

1) Choose a listing site.
   a) There are several websites out there for people who want to sell their hair.
   b) Spend time looking through each website to determine which one is the right fit for you.
   c) Two of the most popular websites for selling hair are:
      i) BuyandSellHair.com
      ii) OnlineHairAffair.com
2) Once you have chosen which site you will sell your hair on, you need to prepare your listing.
   a) Increase your chance of a sale with several photos and a good description.
   b) Make sure to include the length of hair that you are offering for sale.
   c) Include details about your hair, like color and texture.
   d) Include how often you wash your hair and if you use any styling products.
   e) Potential buyers will want to know if you eat well, smoke or drink.
3) Set a price.
   a) Look through other listings on the website to get an idea of what the fair market value of your hair is.
   b) Be sure to compare your hair to those similar to yours.

c) Prices in the high hundreds to the low thousands are very common.
4) Make your sale.
   a) Once you have a buyer, prepare to cut and ship your hair according to the request of the buyer.
   b) Make sure to braid the cut hair and secure both ends with some kind of bands.
   c) Do not cut and/or ship your hair until you have received full payment from the buyer.
   d) Most sellers use PayPal to receive payments.
   e) You might also consider purchasing delivery confirmation and insurance options on your package. If your package is lost, you will be monetarily reimbursed by the post office.

#28: A Crazy Idea:

How to Make Emergency Money Selling Breast Milk

I admit it. This one is a bit strange. Most folks, including me, probably wouldn't bother, but some creative souls are making money selling their breast milk.

As you know, many doctors recommend that breast-feeding is the optimal nutrition for babies. Apparently they are able to digest breast milk much easier than formula. Breast milk contains leukocytes, fats, proteins, vitamins and carbohydrates. As weird as it may sound, a lactating woman can sell her excess breast milk for an average of $2.50 per ounce. Some places offer more; other places offer less per ounce.

Only The Breast is a website that allows a woman to make a profile and place ads to sell their breast milk. Once you join the website, you can create your ad for free. You must be as specific as possible when creating the ad.

The ads to buy breast milk will be categorized by age of the babies: zero to two months, two to six months, and six to twelve months. Buyers are going to want to know: Are you disease-free? Have you had a recent blood test performed? What were the results? How do you store the breast milk? How will the breast milk be shipped to them? Many buyers may also request a written letter from your doctor stating that your breast milk will not risk the health of the child ingesting it.

You can choose to sell to local buyers or to ship your frozen milk to long-distance buyers.

Another option for selling your breast milk is to reach out to milk banks, such as Mother's Milk Cooperative. This company pays $1 per ounce of breast milk. You must complete an extensive screening process before you are approved to submit your breast milk. If you are accepted, your milk will be tested for safety and quality along with adulterants before the breast milk is processed for use. You must wait three months after the birth of your baby before selling your breast milk. After your milk has been received and has passed the screening process, payments will be made by direct deposit into a checking or savings account. You must fill out a direct deposit form and fax it back to the company. Payment is issued ninety days after they receive your milk. Regardless of how many shipments you have sent in, each shipment has a ninety-day pay period. The money you make from selling your milk is considered Miscellaneous Income, and you will receive a 1099 at the end of the year.

So, if you've got milk, you may just get paid! Who knew?

Websites:

http://www.onlythebreast.com

http://www.mothersmilk.coop

Conclusion

There are things you can do to avoid a financial crisis before one arises. Most people are not prepared financially to deal with such a crisis, so here are things you can do to minimize or even avoid one before it happens:

1) Start an emergency fund. Decide on the amount of money you want to have set aside in your emergency fund. Add to the fund until you have reached your desired amount and only use the money for emergencies. Having an emergency fund can reduce the stress and panic of a financial crisis.
2) Stay out of debt. Try your best to avoid credit card debt. Limit the amount of open credit cards and other small loans if possible. If you have a lot of debt, and you are faced with a financial crisis, your finances can spin out of control very fast.
3) Have insurance. Insurance can be expensive but will pay off in the long run. You should at least make sure that you are covered by a health plan. Also make sure that you have sufficient insurance on your vehicle and home. This way, if a financial emergency should occur with either of these things, they will be covered by your insurance policy. Also it may be a good idea to look into disability insurance in case you are hurt or become sick and are not able to continue with your current employment.

BONUS

Job Boards and Emergency Moneymaking Websites and Blogs

Job Boards

Indeed.com:

In Business Since: 2004
Vice Job Fee: N/A
Apply By: Profile

Suggested Emergency Money Categories: Security, Front Desk Officer, Planner/Scheduler, Banquet Server, Assembler

Description: Indeed.com launched in November 2004 and is a very popular and free job search engine available in over fifty countries. This site lists opportunities from thousands of sites, including associations, company career pages, staffing firms, and job boards. Indeed allows job seekers to skip the middleman and apply to positions listed on their site. It also gives job seekers the opportunity to post and store résumés. This company is listed in Austin, TX, and has global offices. If you're searching for part-time, full-time, or emergency income circumstances, Indeed is a great choice.

Website: http://www.indeed.com/

Monster.com:

In Business Since: 1999
Vice Job Fee: N/A
Apply By: Résumé

Suggested Emergency Money Categories: Quality Technician, Part-Time Weekend Receptionist, Weekend Computer Operator, Warehouse Utility Worker, Weekend Bookkeeper

Description: If you're in need of part-time, full-time, or emergency income, Monster is an exceptional option. It is owned and operated by Monster Worldwide, Inc. Formed in 1999 when The Monster Board (TMB) and Online Career Center (OCC) merged, Monster.com has become a very popular employment website. The search engine is third behind Indeed.com and Careerbuilder.com. Monster is used by those individuals seeking work to find job openings that match their skills and geographical location.

In 2008, Monster had over sixty-three million job seekers visit them, listed over one million résumés from job seekers, and had over one million job postings. The company itself has approximately five thousand employees on its payroll in thirty-six countries with its primary offices located in Weston, Maine.

Website: http://www.monster.com/

SnagAJob.com:

In Business Since: 2000
Vice Job Fee: N/A
Apply By: Profile

Suggested Emergency Money Categories: General Laborer, Event Coordinator/Driver, Pastry Chef, Arcade Attendant, Retail Sales Associate, Online Survey Taker

Description: SnagAJob has seventy million registered job seekers who have utilized this platform. The mobile solution platform makes it easy for workers to find jobs and for employers to locate workers and to offer mobile solutions for each step in the hiring process. SnagAJob's headquarters are located in Virginia with offices in Richmond and Arlington. According to *Fortune* magazine, SnagAJob has been listed as one of the Great Places to Work in the Best Small & Medium Workplaces for over eight years. In 2015, SnagAJob was also recognized by the *Washingtonian* magazine as a Great Place to Work.

Website: http://www.snagajob.com/

TotalJobs.com:

In Business Since: 1999
Vice Job Fee: N/A
Apply By: Profile

Suggested Emergency Money Categories: Solutions Architect, Construction Manager, Back-End Developer, Data Applications Engineer

Description: TotalJobs Group is a hodgepodge of online job boards in the UK. They actually have six recruitment sites, including RetailChoice.com for the retail industry, TotalJobs.com for jobs spanning multiple industries, Caterer.com and Catererglobal.com for the hospitality industry, CareerStructure.com for the construction industry, and CWJobs.co.uk for IT. The TotalJobs Group excels in helping job seekers find work and helping recruiters fill their vacancies in part-time, full-time, and temporary job opportunities.

Website: http://www.totaljobs.com/

Jobs2Careers.com:

In Business Since: 1985
Vice Job Fee: N/A
Apply By: Profile

Suggested Emergency Money Categories: Deckhand, Quarry Laborer, Supervisor, Overnight Health Center Manager, Massage Therapist, RN Supervisor

Description: Jobs2Careers is one of the top online platforms for locating high-value team members and high-quality jobs. Using Jobs2Careers is as simple as it can be. Select a job type and location, and instantly results are ready to review. Whether seeking part-time or full-time work, the site provides job seekers with free access from their desktop or smartphone to locate listings for everything from small jobs to big careers.

Website: http://www.jobs2careers.com/

SimplyHired.com:

In Business Since: 2003
Vice Job Fee: N/A

Apply By: Profile

Suggested Emergency Money Categories: Banquet Server, Street Team Squad Member, Brewer, Senior Specialist, Steward, Librarian, Consumer Lending Processor

Description: With its own mobile application and recruitment advertising network, SimplyHired.com takes part-time, full-time, and temporary job searches to a new level. The site pulls together job listings from every corner of the Internet and then organizes those jobs on its website, phone app, and social network. Job searching is quick and easy as seekers search listings using key words and a specific location to filter results and zero in on the ideal jobs. Prospective employers can leverage results by using premium listing services offered by SimplyHired.com.

Website: http://www.simplyhired.com/

Job-Less.info:

In Business Since: 2000
Vice Job Fee: N/A
Apply By: Profile

Suggested Emergency Money Categories: Weekend Editor, Receptionist, Counselor

Description: Job-less.info is a search engine for jobs in the USA. This site offers a condensed search engine, focused solely on job opportunities within the United States. In a straightforward approach, Job-less.info provides part-time, full-time, and temporary job seekers a hassle-free access to thousands of job listings from all across the country. Key word and location search filters allow the seeker to find just the right job in just the right location.

Website: http://www.job-less.info/

Laborready.com:

In Business Since: 2000
Vice Job Fee: N/A
Apply By: Profile

Description: Labor Ready focuses on placing the right temporary employee in the right job. The major strengths of Labor Ready is its recruiting, screening, and hiring tools to help match construction companies, light industry, and small businesses with the right workers.

For job seekers in need of training and skills, Labor Ready offers training and tools that help expand your options and your resources.

Website: http://www.laborready.com/

Emergency Money Blogs

Scott Alan Turner

Get out of debt faster. Save more money. Retire rich.

Scott is a family man who was living paycheck to paycheck, buying items with credit cards, and had a car payment. He decided it was time for a change and started learning about getting out of debt, saving, and investing. By the age of thirty-five he was debt-free, had no mortgage, and was a self-made millionaire. This is what led him to writing his free How to Save $1,000 in One Week Challenge. There are countless articles available on his blog from things like:

- Making extra money,
- Getting out of debt,
- Budgeting,
- Using debit cards over credit cards,
- Investing,
- Shopping and retail tips,
- Saving for retirement,
- Learning personal finance tips,
- Recognizing scams and rip-offs.

He also has 147 podcasts, which can be listened to on his blog or on iTunes, Google Play Music, and Android devices. Here are just a few of the topics he covers:

- Importance of having a spending plan,
- Reducing grocery bills,
- Importance of savings,
- Avoiding the evil credit cards.

You can also submit questions directly to Scott and subscribe to his monthly newsletter.

Visit Scot's blog here: http://scottalanturner.com/

The Penny Hoarder

The Penny Hoarder is part of the Taylor Media family, one of the fastest-growing digital media companies located in the United States. Their mission is to put more money into their readers' pockets by sharing stories from real people and providing practical tips that anyone can use. Kyle Taylor is the founder and CEO of The Penny Hoarder. He began writing the blog about his adventures in saving and making money. The blog has grown into one of the largest publications on the Internet.

On this blog you will find information on:

- Money Hacks
    - How to save money on cleaning supplies
    - Ways to save money on groceries
    - How to save money on school supplies
    - How to save money while traveling
    - Tricks to managing money
    - How to save money on plane tickets
    - How to manage money
- Working from Home
    - Information about companies hiring people to work from home
    - Additional websites with information about work-from-home jobs
- Budgeting
    - Strategies to make budgeting easier
    - Budgeting mistakes
    - How to make and save money while attending college
    - Teaching your kids about money
- Coupons
    - How to save money using coupons
    - Companies that will send free coupons
    - Places to find free coupons
    - Printable coupons

- Freebies
    - Wedding freebies
    - Teacher freebies
    - Internet freebies
    - Restaurant freebies

All this and much more can be found here:
http://www.thepennyhoarder.com/

Lifehack

Lifehack is a blog that is updated frequently with articles written by a team of contributors. Here you can learn things about money, lifestyle, productivity, work, motivation, technology, family, and relationships.

Here are some of the articles you will find on this blog:

- Money
    - 10 Money-Saving Tips in a Balanced Life
    - How to Pave the Road to Financial Freedom Little by Little
    - 5 Alternative Ways to Make Money
    - 6 Ways to Make More Money as a Freelancer
- Productivity
    - 8 Tasks You Should Be Delegating
    - 4 Mind-Set Changes Successful People Adopt for Unprecedented Success
    - Take the 7-Week Time Management Challenge

This and many more articles can be found here:
http://www.lifehack.org/money?ref=nav-bar-money

Money Crashers

Money Crashers is a blog dedicated to educating people on how to make wise choices about credit and debit, real estate, spending, investing, insurance, and education. They want to make sure that people are no longer targets of financial predators. They want people to manage their money through common sense and self-control. Here are a few of their core principles:

1) Don't spend too much.
2) Do not believe in money myths.
3) Eliminate debt and stay out of debt.
4) Save money to prepare for the unexpected.
5) Be resourceful and open-minded, especially when deciding to take out student loans.
6) Boost your income with creativity and be willing to think outside the box.
7) Keep your investment strategy simple and think long-term.
8) Be knowledgeable about cars, financial products, real estate, and other investment opportunities.
9) Stay away from financial scammers and protect your assets.
10) Always treat your partner or spouse as your financial teammate.
11) If you achieve financial success, give back. It helps others and feels great.

Here you will find ways to manage your money through articles on spending and saving, budgeting, banking, taxes, and insurance. You can also learn the dos and don'ts of using credit cards, how to invest in your retirement, and about the economy. More information can be found here: http://www.moneycrashers.com/

NerdWallet

NerdWallet is a blog that offers objective advice and financial tools so that people understand their options and make the best decisions. The folks here make it easy to find the best deals on credit cards, insurance, and mortgages. They have articles geared toward ways to reduce your monthly payments. They also have an online specialist who you can submit your questions to.

Find out things like:

- What are the best credit cards for 2016
- Credit cards with the best rewards
- Credit cards that offer cash back
- Credit cards with low interest
- Best checking accounts
- Best savings accounts
- Best prepaid debit cards
- Best brokers for beginners
- Best 529 plans
- Best Roth IRA provider
- Find a mortgage refinance lender
- Help from a mortgage broker
- Best private school loans
- Best car loans
- And much more

To read about any of the things mentioned above and so much more, visit: https://www.nerdwallet.com/?trk=nw_gn_4.0

Money Management International

Money Management International is nonprofit credit counseling agency located in the United States. They help people find the solutions they need so that they may achieve financial freedom. They offer help with educational programs, debt management assistance, credit counseling, and bankruptcy. On this website, you will find information about personal finance, financial services, and useful tools.

There are articles and blog posts to help when someone is in financial crisis. Some are:

- Three Steps for Dealing with Significant Medical Bills
- How to Stop Debt Collection Calls

- Financial Goal Setting
- How to Avoid Repossession of Your Car
- How to Recover from a Personal Financial Setback

Along with these articles you can use the webinars, videos, eBooks, and podcasts available here to find additional information on many subjects.

Visit the website here:
https://www.moneymanagement.org/Financial-ducation/Financial-Problems.aspx

My Money Coach

My Money Coach website has a vast amount of information about money. Here you will learn how to save money and make smart financial decisions. This site is about saving people money and educating the public about personal finance.

Here you can use tools to help with money management, budgeting (using a budget calculator and expense tracker), dealing with creditors, and solving debt problems. Along with those tools, you'll also find a huge amount of information about:

- What a budget is,
- Budgeting guidelines,
- How to pay off debt faster,
- How to save money,
- How to save an emergency fund,
- Tips to save money,
- How to save on energy bills,
- How to curb impulse spending,
- How to save on groceries,
- How to teach your kids about handling money better.

On their blog, many posts are about things like overcoming financial problems, identifying any underlying problems causing the financial difficulties, financial priorities, and developing a plan. For more information, visit:

http://www.mymoneycoach.ca/blog/how-to-overcome-financial-problems-difficulties

Dave Ramsey

Dave Ramsey knows what it is like to go from having everything to having nothing. He formed Ramsey Solutions in 1992 so that he could counsel people having financial stress. He has since written six bestsellers on *The New York Times*, *Wall Street Journal*, and *Publishers Weekly* best-sellers' lists. His team consists of over 550 members to help you reach your financial goals. Along with teaching people how to budget their money, he also teaches people how to get out of and stay out of debt. Podcasts and videos are available, and also classes, live events, and tools. Posts on his blog include things like:

- 5 Things Budgeting Taught Me about Myself
- The Truth about Getting out of Debt
- How to Budget an Irregular Income in 3 Easy Steps
- How Do You Save Money on Everyday Expenses?

Many more posts can be read on the seventy-plus pages of his blog. You can read more posts here:

http://www.daveramsey.com/blog?page=1

Suze Orman: Financial Solutions for You

USA Today often refers to Suze Orman as "a force in the world of personal finance." She is a best-selling author, online and magazine columnist, motivational speaker, and a writer/producer. In 2009, she received a Visionary Award from the Council for Economic Education. She was also given a honorary Doctor of Humane Letters degree from the University of Illinois.

On her website, she has a blog that covers topics such as:

- Emergency Fund 101
- Avoid This Costly Refinancing Trap
- Tips to Keep Your Prescription Drug Cost Down
- How to Spend Your Tax Return
- Take Care of Your Family's Financial Fears

These posts and many, many more can be found on her blog. Also you will find books and kits, calculators, and a resource center with advice from Suze regarding debt management, will and trusts, home ownership, financial intimacy, retirement planning, and record keeping. To get more information, visit: http://www.suzeorman.com/

Sense & Centsibility Blog

The Sense & Centsibility Blog is the official blog for LSS Financial Counseling. They aim to teach the public about financial topics that affect everyone. They specialize in financial counseling, helping people facing foreclosure, and assisting with medical and student loan debt.

They have a great "What Is a Financial Emergency?" post. It talks about things that may cause someone to face a financial emergency and things that can be done to prevent a financial emergency from occurring. There are also resources for avoiding scams, plus useful budget calculators, financial links, helpful documents, and a frequently asked question section. To find out more information, visit http://www.lssmn.org/debt/

Quick and Dirty Tips

Quick and Dirty Tips is a website that consists of twenty-two writers/contributors. They write about a large assortment of topics, such as, relationships, pets, health and wellness, education, business, careers, money and finance, house and home, and parenting. Money Girl writes about topics from credit to taxes and everything in between. When you visit the Money and Finance section, you will find articles like:

- Money Management for New Couples
- Credit Q&A: Monitor, Repair & Build Your Credit
- 10 Products to Create Financial Security
- Avoid Spending Mistakes
- What to Do with Extra Money
- Erase Debt
- And much more!

Hundreds of articles are written by the Money Girl to guide you through your financial issues. If you would like to read more of her articles, visit: http://www.quickanddirtytips.com/money-girl.

Emergency Income Streams

About the Author

Kristi Patrice Carter is a wife, mother, author, and serial entrepreneur who loves making active and passive income and helping others do the same. Carter's lifelong goal is to positively impact people's lives, one self-help book at a time.

A force to be reckoned with, Carter earned a Bachelor of Arts in English from the University of Illinois and a Juris Doctorate from Chicago-Kent College of Law and has over seventeen years of experience in the writing industry. She is the author of:

- *Active Income Streams: Side Income Opportunities for Achieving Financial Freedom (Working As Much or As Little as You Desire)*
- *Passive Income Streams: How to Create and Profit from Passive Income Even If You're Cash-Strapped and a Little Bit Lazy (But Motivated)!*

- *Say No to Guilt! The 21 Day Plan for Accepting Your Chronic Illness and Finding Inner Peace and Happiness*
- *Say Yes to Success Despite Your Chronic Illness: 10 Weeks to Overcoming the Obstacles of Chronic Illness and Finally Achieving What You Want in Life!*
- *Wean That Kid: Your Comprehensive Guide to Understanding and Mastering the Weaning Process*
- *I'm a Weaned Kid Now*

www.ingramcontent.com/pod-product-compliance
Lightning Source LLC
Chambersburg PA
CBHW071443180526
45170CB00001B/431